Being Bourne

Martin Bourne

PARTRIDGE
A Penguin Random House Company

To order additional copies of this book, contact
Toll Free 800 101 2657 (Singapore)
Toll Free 1 800 81 7340 (Malaysia)
orders.singapore@partridgepublishing.com

www.partridgepublishing.com/singapore

Preface

Nobody's memory is perfect even if we think it is. My story is in the main from my own recollections and true to the very best of my knowledge.

For at least the last 30 years some members of my family and friends have said to me, Martin you should write a book, after I have told them little stories from my past. Finally while visiting my good friend Tony Smith in England two years ago during a conversation he said, "You have lived quite a life haven't you Martin?" "I suppose I have," I replied. This got me thinking and was the final comment to invigorate my reflections on the possibility of writing my autobiography. The seed was planted, very soon to be germinated on my return to Australia. Needless to say, this is not the story of my life in its entirety, as some stories will always be extremely private.

While every reasonable endeavour has been made to confirm the truthfulness and dependability of the information contained in my memoirs, my apologies for any incorrect name spellings and permissions that could not be sort where I have felt it was necessary from persons contactable. All events are subject to the absolute minimum extent of literary licence.

I sincerely hope that my readers who don't know me take some pleasure in my exploits and philosophies, it's been a long and exciting and sometimes arduous journey. The changes I have experienced have been astonishing and captivating to say the least.

For any readers who have shared the times with me over, in some cases, many years through some of my adventures or even my working life, hello again and I hope you enjoy reminiscing some of our moments together. For quite a number of years I have had the notions of gathering everyone I know and knew for one massive reunion, but unfortunately the logistics and cost were too problematic, so this was the next best quest.

Many experiences of my life over the years are not included in this book for a variety of reasons. However I must stress that they have unquestionably influenced my thoughts on the human condition. I'm not normally one to shy off from making waves or rocking the boat, but this must be where I draw the line! Maybe in 20 years from now.

My apologies if there is any content that you may find slightly distasteful or unpleasant, as some words or phrases I believe to be necessary for certain stories. Some names have been changed to protect the privacy of certain persons. Also some of the places have been left out for the same reasons.

Foreword

Martin was born in Surrey but very shortly afterwards was taken to Upper Norwood to be picked up and brought home to West Dulwich to be raised by his new family. Staying around that area he worked hard and took on various and sometimes multiple jobs to see his family through difficult times. He had a passion for scuba diving and flying light aircraft later on when he had the opportunity. Martin has four children, three stepchildren and twelve grandchildren and one great grandchild.

He has always faced his fears of the unknown with a determination to conquer anything he sees as a challenge. One of his biggest and oldest hurdles has been his lack of education due to his battle with dyslexia. He has never been a confident reader or writer but has persevered his entire life and because of his desire to leave a legacy to his family, both living and for future generations who may just wonder what Martin Bourne did with his life, he decided to write this biography.

Having an extraordinary memory for faces and names he has included many friends, family and some mere acquaintances and hopes word will get around to as many people as possible who may be curious enough to read and enjoy his reminisces.

Although Martin loves his home country deeply and maintains he will always only be a British citizen, he finds himself on the other side of the world in Western Australia where he now lives with his third wife. His wish to regularly return to England to see his loved ones will hopefully continue until the time comes for him to maybe spend longer periods living in the UK.

Being Bourne

A true account of my life with a few
Historical facts

ӿ

A Bourne legacy for my children and
grandchildren for the rest of time.

ӿ

Writing this manuscript has inspired me to do
even more in my life however long it may be.

ӿ

I believe the reason my memories are so imprinted and
long lasting, is due to not being afraid to tell my little
stories to so many people about all of my antics and
adventures, which I am sure reinforces the memory.

ӿ

Nobody can restrict the things life does to us!
We can only try to preserve the good qualities we retain

MB

Some of my inner most thoughts

*Occasionally in life we may make some wrong
decisions that can't be put right.
We can only attempt to learn from them!*

ⵝ

*Even if only a handful of people hold my dearest and most
vivid moments in written form, a few of my cherished
escapades may be talked about in the distant future.*

ⵝ

*Memories are immortal if preserved
They are a precious gift in a space that will one day
cease to exist hurling them all in to oblivion.*

ⵝ

*Without this manuscript all of the things I have seen
and done in my life will vanish like tears in a stream.*

MB

Contents

The Saga Begins
1944-1960

Time to grow up
1960-1975

Ready for Anything
1975 - 2014

Chapter 1

Whatever Next

Mum and my older sisters, Margaret, Janet, Lesley and their dog Prince, were in their home when the Germans dropped incendiary bombs onto their top floor flat in Dalton Street, West Norwood, London, which was situated over a hardware shop that stored huge tanks of paraffin oil! Mum and Marg tried desperately to extinguish the fires but had to give up and flee in case the flames reached the tanks below.

Unfortunately, Prince went back looking for Dad – who was on duty with the ambulance service at the time, so not there – and died in the blaze. They all made their way to a nearby large warehouse opposite Dalton Street. It belonged to H Day and Son – a removal company and furniture store – for that night. Then they were moved to Carnac School in Carnac Street until they could be rehoused. After only two days the local council resettled them into an old three story Victorian house at 108 Rosendale Road, West Dulwich, London only half a mile from their old flat. While living there the bombs continued to drop for I don't know how long, but this house received quite a bit of structural damage.

My sisters were then evacuated to Cornwall in the West Country of England. After a while the eldest of the girls Margaret or Marg as we called her came back to Mum and Dad in London, Janet or Jane and Lesley or Les followed when it was safe.

Then one day late in 1944, a friend of the family, known to us as Aunt Mary, told Mum and Dad about a baby boy whose mother was going to have to give him up. They agreed to take this blue-eyed blond package and bring him up as one of their family. My sisters came to pick me up and take me to my new home.

This is where my story starts, I was that baby and with the love and care of my family, I am here to tell the tale of my life.

I was born towards the end of World War II on December 3, 1944, at a nursing home in Byfleet, Surrey. About ten days later my birth mother, gave me away to my new Dad, William T Bourne – Bill – and Mum, Margaret K Bourne – Peg – at 108 Rosendale Road, West Dulwich, London. This is where I stayed with my three older sisters, Marg, Jane and Les, later when I was 18 months old, a brother, William – Bill was born. My name changed from Martin Osborne to Martin Bourne, all unofficially of course.

This was all happening while the Germans were sending the deadly V1 (Doodlebugs) and V2 Rockets over London. Some of these were diverted from their original target (London) due to misinformation sent unknowingly to the Germans by the British Intelligence, unfortunately these bombs landed around the Dulwich area, where I lived as a tiny baby. The bombing finally stopped on March 29 1945.

My very earliest memories, when I was two, were of being taken to a shop in West Norwood, where I stood on a chair and had my photograph taken. I had a strong feeling that I had been there before. I still have a photograph of that moment. It must have been around that time that I first saw vast amounts of snow when being helped out of our home's back door by a male family member, it may have been Dad's younger brother Uncle Ken. The snow was up to my knees, and went into my wellington boots. Marg reminds me that I took my boot off and while emptying the snow from it, I placed my little foot down in the snow only to then put it back into my boot now completely covered in snow.

Martin aged 2 at the photographers

I must have been only three years old which makes it 1947 when it was the coldest winter ever at minus 21° Fahrenheit, which is minus 29.4 Celsius also it was Christmas time. I was being shown that the top of the milk – the cream – had been pushed a good inch out of the bottle with the gold foil lid still on top of the cream, because the milk had been frozen by the freezing weather. When I was back inside and sat at the breakfast table the cream was then removed and put on my porridge.

Marg and her good friend Ruby Kimpton took me to London Zoo in Regents Park. My transport most of the time was a cumbersome grey pushchair which the Zoo loaned to visitors. I'll never forget the first time I saw an elephant and experienced their smell, elephants in picture books don't smell! Marg told me that while traveling on a top deck of a London bus, when going over a bridge and looking out of the window at the river, I turned with a look of surprise and said out loud "'Oo done all that?" apparently I'd never seen so much water in my short life.

We all lived in an old, four storey, Victorian house with eleven rooms. For the first nine years of my life, we had people living on the top floor. First there was Fanny Fowlkes and her husband Jimmy, who liked a bit of a drink and kept a bucket or chamber pot under their bed. He seems to have missed it so often that it seeped through to the ceiling below causing a yellow stain.

Apparently I couldn't say my 'tr' sounds and used an 'f' sound so tree became 'fee' and so on. Fanny used to ask me to say truck for a bit of fun! Ha ha.

Then there was Mr and Mrs Farmer. He was a tall, thin Englishman and she was a full-figured over-made up German lady whose perfume still permeates my nostrils when I think of her. The Farmers had a middle section of our garden for a while, thank goodness we got it back later on. There were two old nurses who were on the next floor down, a Miss Clunen, who apparently used to sing to me and Miss Rangecroft. At one point I believe an old lady, Mrs Craig lived in the front basement room. After she left we used it as a sitting room.

On my fifth birthday I came downstairs in the morning to find Mum and Dad – and most likely the rest of the family – standing by the kitchen table with a big present for me. It was such an exciting moment and everyone was waiting for me! After standing on a chair to reach, I unwrapped it and to my astonishment, it was a big red box. I opened it to find it full of real carpenter's tools. The feeling of joy was unbeatable. My dad had painted all the wooden handles on the tools red, the same colour as the box. The tools were sharp chisels, planes, and saws, Dad planned to teach me carpentry from that early age and that's exactly what he did. He started by showing me how to sharpen and care for my tools, and later simple joints and construction methods. This stood me in good stead for my uncertain future.

One day Dad presented me with a wooden scooter that he had made for me, painted red of course. I gave it quite a bashing, why, I don't quite understand even now, but I would drive the scooter into the kitchen wall and because it wouldn't go through the wall I'd get frustrated and very angry until I broke it. Dad would painstakingly repair it, once with a steel bracket, I should be ashamed to say that I still broke it. My poor family, what they had to endure.

Dad took me for a walk up Rosendale Road to a small shop. He opened the door and with his hand placed gently on my back, eased me forward and encouraged me to go through and into the room, cautiously I obeyed. When inside, I saw there was a man standing between two large leather covered chairs. In front of these were two very ornate mirrors and lots of shelves all around the walls which were full of a variety of interesting bottles, scissors, treacherous looking cut throat razors and other items I had never seen before. It was, of course, my first visit to the barbers, Angel's barber shop to be precise. As I was only a little lad, he put an extremely well-worn plank of wood across the arms of one chair for me to sit on. He started to cut my hair with his noisy machine which caused a tingle up and down my spine as his trimmer skimmed up the back of my neck. After my haircut he gave me a sweet as a reward 'for being so brave!' Dad often took me into Carter's sweet shop next door, to get more sweets for Bill, as we didn't always have our hair cut at the same time. Bill used to love the little fruit salads and blackjacks which were four for a penny.

Then came the time to go to my first school, Rosendale Road School. It was a one mile walk from home, and I was not aware of who walked with me but I was terrified that I would be left behind at this large, unfamiliar building forever and how I cried. It was so traumatic and I put that down to previous experience of the time I needed to be put in care for two weeks when my brother was born. After a while I was fine and soon made friends. As I was reluctant to go to school every day, I'm told that Dad often took me in the mornings, with my wooden scooter, and returned with it to pick me up in the afternoons.

The school was situated near the railway line, which was up on an embankment overlooking the building, and the teachers had to stop talking each time steam trains went thundering by. We could each feel the vibrations through our feet. Sometimes British Railway workers set light to the embankment if it was overgrown, there must have been a plant like cannabis or the like because the smoke was so aromatic and intoxicating. Later in my life this scent turned up on occasions if somebody was having a burn up which immediately took me flying back to my school days.

One day Mum came to collect me half-way through the day because Uncle Ken had come home. With her kind and friendly face, Mum put her head around the classroom door and said to the teacher, "Can I take Martin home?" I'm sure Ken was still in the RAF when he used to bring lots of sweets for us, including a great big bag of coffee creams. They were kept in an old sideboard in the living room and by the time we had eaten them, over what seemed like weeks, I felt quite sick, not wanting to ever have another coffee cream chocolate.

Ken was a cook in the RAF and always bought us stuff from the Navy, Army and Air Force Institute. One day he brought a barrel of grapes packed in small pea-size pieces of cork, it was kept in the old pantry opposite the kitchen door in the hallway. On another occasion, Ken parked an RAF Queen Mary aircraft transporter outside our home. It took up the space of three houses. Me and other kids from the street played football and cricket in the trailer. It was a blue-grey vehicle with high battened sides, which made it safe for little tykes like us to kick around in. Ken used to help me up into the cab which seemed so high in those days.

Bedford OX Tractor Unit and Queen Mary Trailer,
the type Uncle Ken parked outside our house

Uncle Ken loved to tell the story of when he was cooking
for the spitfire pilots, after they had come down from dog
fights over the south of England to refuel their aeroplanes at
Biggin Hill Airfield and RAF Base. Apparently his kitchen
was destroyed by a German aircraft, so he had to set up a
makeshift kitchen next to the runways. With a beaming smile
on his face he would start to tell us how one day while making
a Spotted Dick suet pudding, a Gerry aircraft came down
firing his guns and shot all of the currents out of his freshly
made Spotted Dick!

Another person we all called uncle was Uncle Ray, who was
a Homeopathic Doctor and drove a grey soft-topped Opel car.
He used to come to the house quite a lot and would give me
some kind of powder wrapped in a piece of paper of which
the taste I still have a vague memory. Mum and Dad told me

once that he had a car accident and actually drove himself to hospital with a broken neck!

One morning when only five I thought I was going somewhere nice when Mum took me to an unknown place. We sat on a bench seat with lots of boys around my age, who kept disappearing from one end, it all seemed like a game to me, until it was my turn. Suddenly a tall, thin man with a white mask over his face and peering over his spectacles, took my hand and lead me into another room with big bright lights. By this time I realised Mum had already gone and it was only later in life that I realized why she vanished so quickly. She was afraid I would have kicked up such a stink, being so scared and with good cause as I was about to undergo one of the most traumatic experiences of my life, I kid you not.

My tonsils were about to be ripped out of my throat, the surgeon's mask and the shiny metal tool in his hand made him extremely frightening as he hovered over my mouth. I fought the gas they administered, with its ghastly, almost sweet, smell of rubber mask and gas, until they couldn't give me any more. Mum was told that while I was conscious but semi-paralysed, during the operation, I had kicked the surgeon in the face. I was pleased to hear that. I had trouble coping with, and I complained bitterly about a loose piece of skin flapping at the back of my throat every time I breathed in and out it was absolutely horrible.

A couple of days were spent eating jelly and ice cream, which was soothing, before going home. Twenty odd years later at an examination of my throat by Dr T G Skinner – who stayed as my doctor until I was in my late thirties – found that the back of my throat was a mess of scar tissue due to botched tonsillectomy.

While I was at Rosendale School, I made a few friends, in particular Michael Evans and Brian Nuttall who lived in Peabody Buildings at the Brockwell Park end of Rosendale Road. I loved going to Michael's house after school for tea, his mum was a nice Welsh lady and I enjoyed having sandwiches and cake with them. When walking back home, I would have to go under the railway bridges and that was where an old, dirty-faced tramp, who seemed to live there, startled me on some occasions, a little spooky for a six year old. Michael, Brian and I frequently went over to the railway embankment hunting for grass snakes and lizards, after climbing a rickety old fence. The first time I held a lizard I was fascinated by the movement of their watchful, tiny eyes and the structure of their delicate feet.

My first ever experience of a music class was also at Rosendale School where we were given an instrument to learn. All the kids were given trumpets, flutes and drums, then along came the teacher and handed me a piece of bent metal, as I thought, of course it was a triangle. I was so terribly disappointed after looking at all the other more intricate and challenging instruments. No wonder I always strived to acquire more glamorous toys in the future.

When I was around six going on seven, my pals Martin John, who lived over Marion's the drapers shop and Michael Vesty who lived on the opposite side of the road and I would often play with a homemade trolley or box cart as they were often called. We took turns to push each other as fast as we could up and down our local streets. Then a disaster happened as it quite often did. I was being pushed fast and getting a bit close to the roadside so I pulled on the steering a little too hard and rolled off the trolley onto the road. Unfortunately I went under a motorbike going past at that moment. It went over my leg and hurt like hell. Luckily, we were near my own house and as I was being carried there by the man who ran over me, I looked at my leg with the wheel mark across it and was horrified to notice it was quite squashed, which was the scariest part. This had a lasting impression on me. Do we learn from our mistakes? Not always I think.

Sometimes even at this tender age my pals and I would venture as far as West Dulwich railway station and watch the trains. My first recollection of travelling on a steam engine, was from West Dulwich to London. The vibration of nonstop trains went through my feet up from the shuddering platform and the air pressure they created almost knocked me over, but it was incredibly exhilarating. I marvelled at the sensation of power when the screeching sound of steam was released from the pistons.

After a year at Rosendale School I changed to Elmcourt School in Elmcourt Road, Tulse Hill, I liked it better there. I loved drawing and was good at it. I would get nine out of ten for most of my work. Clay modelling was another enjoyable craft and I soon found my tactile talents improving, which was just as well, as I was totally useless at most academic subjects like Maths and English.

One time after it had snowed all night, I arrived at school and with my friends, started to compact the snow in a long line. The idea was to make a slide. We soon had a nice long slipway. After quite a few successful runs, the bell went but I had to have my last go, so I took a good strong run at the start of the slipway only to lose my balance halfway along.

Because of my haste, disaster struck! I fell backwards and bashed the back of my head, although it hurt I felt ok, then walked back to the classroom. While walking back I felt a little strange, as if something was missing. When sitting in the classroom I started to cry. The teacher noticed and asked me what was wrong.

"I don't know" I replied. "I can't remember saying goodbye to my Mum, or walking to school this morning."

The teacher asked my friend Michael Thompson to take me home. I had suffered amnesia and can't remember if I was taken to the doctors!

My best friend at that time was Robin Myoscoff because we seemed to have the same way of thinking. Another, Victor Page, had a fantastic soprano voice and was always asked to sing for us even though most of the boys would laugh at his very high pitch and said he sounded like a girl. Michael Thompson, Victor Gunn and David Allan, were more friends I played around the streets with while we walk home.

One game we would play was 'knock down Ginger' where one of us had to knock at a stranger's door and count to ten before running away. John Byard was a great pal too, I saw him about forty nine years later, in a Macro store, when I recognised him immediately and greeted him. We chatted briefly and I haven't seen him since. His dad, Ted Byard, was a bus driver at West Norwood Bus Garage and knew Dennis Hill, my brother in-law. Apparently Ted, being a Welshman, of course had a very good singing voice and sang at new Chatsworth Church, Idmiston Road on Sunday Services. The old Chatsworth Church which stood on the same ground was hit by a V2 Rocket, in the war and was completely flattened.

Quite often we would play conkers at school, after collecting our horse chestnuts. We pushed a meat skewer through the middle of the beautiful shiny brown nut, then pass a length of string through the hole and knot it. Taking it in turns, we swung our conker at the opponent's conker, if you missed, it was tough luck. That was your go. The idea was to smash your opponent's conker to smithereens.

We might play marbles instead if we had a fairly smooth surface to roll these colourful glass spheres on. Sometimes we played for an opponent's favourite marble, which might be an alley (short for alabaster), a name associated with a larger marble.

Other days, cigarette cards were the choice. So out came the cards, thanks to the smokers of the world, they were found in certain packets of cigarettes namely Players Navy Cut or Woodbines. The cards had pictures on the front and usually a write-up on the reverse side. They might be about famous footballers, motorcars, racing cars, wildflowers or even household hints. The idea of the game was to stand your cards against the wall, then the opponent flicked his card from a fair distance to try to hit your card and knock it down flat on the ground, he would then win the one which you had chosen to risk. These games were not limited to school, the roads around our homes were much safer than today and were a great playground. Occasionally cars such as the Standard Vanguard, Austin Seven, Humber and Hillman would stop play.

One project I created at Elmcourt at eight or nine, was to make a nativity scene in hand-painted clay with the three Kings and baby Jesus in his crib. Sarah-Jane my niece informed me these models were still in the display cabinet near the entrance when she went to the same school about sixteen years later. The school had a name change and a location change by this time.

Two years later at this school, I would sit my 11 plus exam and not being able to read the questions, I obviously failed. I was told that Mum tried to stop me having to sit through it, and it was later realised I suffered from Dyslexia. Mum tried unsuccessfully to get me placed in a new school. She was told that the only school that would take me would be an ESN – educationally subnormal – school. Mum would not have that at all.

Chapter 2

Adventures at Last

On the occasional Sunday, my sisters would take Bill and me to Westgate on the steam train for a day trip just to go to the beach! Bill and I had the usual fun that kids do, like building sand castles and digging holes. This became a little boring, so I began to dig bigger and deeper holes on each visit and moved closer to the sea, then cut a channel to allow the sea to surge into the hole. My urge to dig down deeper and deeper and form a tunnel to link with a previous hole this would cause the sand to collapse on top of me most of the time. I think this is where my passion for tunnelling began and Mum always expressed to me and to others that I had no physical fear.

Once I took home a crab in my bucket with a little water and when I got home I put the bucket containing the crab in the back garden and forgot about it, as you do. The crab died, obviously, and how it stunk!

I loved being with my sisters on these excursions at this stage in my life but best behaviour wasn't always maintained, subsequently it was nice to be with my gang without being told off, if I put a foot out of line.

I would often be seen kicking around the streets with a group of other kids, namely Johnny Hiberd, Colin Masters, Brian Saunders, and Malcolm Hall. We were always getting into old bomb damaged houses and bomb sites and we explored what would have been about 100 Rosendale Road - which was demolished a few years later - when I was around seven or eight. We cautiously climbed up the damaged staircase, and I noticed the smell of the dust it was so acrid as it was in most old deserted buildings, it was also so stirring rooting around looking into cupboards. In one cupboard I came across a round tin about 2 ½" in diameter and after twisting the lid off I was faced with tin foil wrapped discs. With the undoing of the foil, I found chocolate rounds segmented in to quarters consequently, me being me, I ate some. It tasted a little bitter but that wasn't going to deter me. After I got home Mum saw me hiding the tin behind my back and asked me for it. She looked at the tin and was horrified to find it contained rat poison! The reaction on her face, as she was informed of this, was enough to alarm me into an anxious confession of telling her I had eaten some. I don't know what happened next, but I do know that shortly after, I had chronic diarrhoea. Consequently it was a good job that my sisters would take me out occasionally in the safety of their care and away from such dangers.

Marg took me to places like Joe Lyons Tea Rooms in Brixton Road, Brixton. Sometimes Marg's friend Ruby Kimpton came with us. Ruby was an attractive woman who wore lots of makeup. We would have tea and cake or ice cream before or after walking around the shops, hundreds and hundreds of shops! Marg also took me to the movies, mostly to the old Regal Cinema in Norwood Road, after calling in to Gordon's sweet shop opposite. Once seated, I would be entranced by such films as 'The Dam Busters' with Richard Todd, 'Reach for the Sky' with Kenneth Moore, 'The Red Beret' with Alan Ladd, 'Old Yeller' with Fess Parker and 'The Cockleshell Heroes' with José Ferrer and Anthony Newley. It all seems so long ago now but it made an impression throughout my life.

I was taken on a tram for the first time in West Norwood, I can still see the green tinted glass at the rear window, also the sound as it started to move off with a 'yong yung yong' sound which gradually went up in pitch. The clatter they made was very different to a train. The trams stopped running when I was about seven or eight. After a few years of them being stopped. The road workers removed all the wooden blocks – teak I believe – which had been secured in place with tar. These blocks held the rails in place and were then left at the roadside. One day Dad and I collected as many as we could carry home at a time for the home fire. Because of the tar they burned very well although a little smelly and the chimney was always catching alight, Mum would throw a hand full of salt on the fire to calm down the flames. She was always saving the day.

I was occasionally distracted from my adventures with my mates, with a different kind of adventure. An old friend of the family, who we knew as Uncle Alec, who was a slimly built man, most times was smartly dressed and always smoked Senior Service cigarettes. I must have been around six and while I was sitting on his knee one day, he was squeezing my upper arm and to this day his words ring in my head as he said to Mum, "Have you seen this boys muscles Peg?" From this simple comment I was devoted to personal physical strength and fitness.

Alec used to keep an old Triumph motorbike at the side of the front steps at 108, which Bill and I often played on. One day I opened the fuel cap and peed into the petrol tank. I never remember Alec ever using this bike but sometime Later, on opening the fuel tank, Alec said, "What the heck is that smell!" after a week or two he jested and remarked that the bike seemed to go faster after that. Alec kept his main motorbike, the famous Panther (which I travelled on many times) and accommodated it for some time down by the side of the railway arches next to the bridge at the Brockwell Park end of Rosendale Road.

When Uncle Alec used to leave our house on his motor bike, after visiting us, Michael Vesty's little dog Bingo used to chase him nipping at his heels. Alec used to say he had to reach a speed of 28mph before Bingo gave up.

From when I was about seven, Alec would pick me up from home and take me out for the day. We would go to Margate to visit his Mum, which was a journey of seventy two miles (116km) with no crash helmet or leathers. Sometimes it was freezing cold on my hands and especially around my ears, I dread to think where I would be now if we came off the bike at seventy or eighty miles an hour. My feet wouldn't reach the footrests at first so I had to put one foot on the hooter, the other on the tool box, sometimes my toe would touch the spokes of the rear wheel and give me a fright. Alec showed me that I was wearing the paint off where my feet were rubbing.

We would also go to see his brother who owned a sweet shop in Margate and made his own rock. He used to cut off a piece of for me rock while it was still soft, it was chewy like soft toffee with a fruity flavour, I loved it so much of course if I took some home for Bill it hardened before getting there. Then it was time to go home, winter or summer rain, wind and snow, we were certainly an all-weather team Alec and I.

Richmond in Surrey is another place that Alec and I would venture, on the banks of the River Thames. He would pitch his small tent only a few yards from the water's edge, it was extremely exciting. I changed into my swimming trunks and cautiously slipped into the water where it was shallow, as I hadn't quite mastered my swimming technique. Meanwhile Alec was pumping his Primus stove preparing for a cup of tea and some cake or even a meal. I could see the fish in the shallow water swimming around my feet, and could feel them nibbling at my toes, I didn't know why they weren't afraid of me although I have been told many times in my life that I have a way with wild creatures. Then I caught my first ever fish with my bare hands it was an exhilarating experience, I think it was a small trout. Alec found an old kettle laying around the river bank and put some river water in it to keep my fish alive until we decided what to do with it. I climbed out of the water and with my towel, dried myself off then had a cuppa with the goodies Alec had prepared for us, another wonderful event.

Back home at 108, we always had gallons of pillar box red and battleship grey paint which was used all over the house, courtesy of Uncle Ken again. At one time Jane painted all the skirting boards, doors and architraves in my bedroom with red paint and lots of children holding hands in white paint. On the door panels she painted a different nursery rhyme scene like Little Miss Muffet and the spider, and little Jack Horner, Humpty Dumpty and Jack and Jill. Jane went to Chelsea art school and among other things she would paint our portraits, which I thought was so clever. My bedroom was a nice big room with an old Victorian fireplace and working gas lamps each side of it, complete with their very delicate mantles. At one stage in my life we were without electricity, gas and candles were our only lighting source at night. The hissing sound from the gas lamps was very calming and actually helped me sleep.

Even the street lighting was gas, a man used to walk down our street just before darkness set in. I watched him with interest from Mum and Dad's bedroom window as he raised his pole, turned on the gas and lit each lamp as he went. Then in the morning he would pass by turning them off again. It was comforting to stand at the window at night and just look at the shop fronts and roofs opposite, or see how many cars went by in a given time, which wasn't many in the early fifties. Sometimes it might be pouring with rain and I would poke my head out to feel the rain on my face, it felt so refreshing summer or winter. This was all very well until Mum or Dad came up and told me to shut the window, because the floor was getting soaked. I did as they asked and closed it, but only to leave the window about four inches from shut just enough to press my face against the window frame so I could still feel the fresh air over my nose and eyes. This had a stimulating effect on my whole being.

It was such a reassuring sight when on some evenings after dark I would sit and look out of Mum's bedroom window at the shops opposite. Out of the corner of my eye I saw a shadow which gradually transformed into our local policemen on foot patrol. If there was a moon on some nights I would see a flash of silver from his chromed helmet and epaulette badges. He was checking all the shop doors slowly and methodically, also pressing his face to the glass windows to check inside with his torch, for any signs of movement.

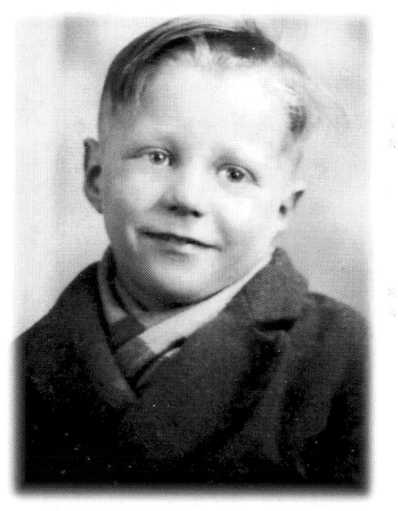

Martin dressed for winter at about 7 years old.

Jane told us one day that her friend was coming to visit us from France, her name was Claude. Jane spent a little time teaching Bill and I how to say good morning and other simple words in French. When Claude finally came she bought us presents like decorative fruits made from marzipan, in particular I received a little plastic man with a parachute and had lots of fun throwing it from one of the top windows then watching it glide gracefully down to earth.

What was the small basement room or scullery, Dad turned into a workshop, here I had my opportunity to use my tools to a greater extent. There he started to teach me his trade as a cabinet maker. Of course there was more to making things, I had to learn to clear up after myself, putting sawdust, shavings and tools away, every time I finished for the day. When I was around twelve years old I made doll's furniture for my niece Sarah-Jane, in particular a tiny sideboard that I copied from one we had in our living room. Dad used to bring home off-cuts of plywood and Rexine (vinyl-like fabric) from his workshop at Decca Record Company, Brixton where he was employed as a cabinet maker.

I loved and appreciated my Dad teaching me woodwork among other things were the times he would hit his finger with a hammer and a very quick 'bugger!' would come from his lips followed by sucking his finger. Being a carpenter most of my working life, I can now appreciate this word and it definitely helps.

I also liked to learn things by myself, often the hard way, roller skating was one such thing to perfect. After quite a short time I was doing somersaults on roller skates, of course the skates I had weren't with nice rubber wheels, they were iron and made a hell of a racket but nonetheless it was great fun and people could hear you coming and get out of your way.

Our kitchen had an old black iron range built into the chimney breast, complete with back boiler and pipes running up to a galvanized hot water tank, this used to bubble and groan as the water heated up. The stove had two hot plates on the top, and an oven which in the early days Mum cooked in. On occasions when I was older I had the job of polishing it with black lead, it was so nice and had an almost silk like shiny surface when I had finished. Bill and I spent many a time toasting our bread in front of it, we seemed to spend a great deal of time stoking and poking fires, sometimes we put plasticine on a stick and watched it melt – it did have quite an unpleasant smell.

We had a wooden clothes dryer fixed to the kitchen ceiling, which we lowered with a rope and pulley system, when the sash line wore out, it was another job for yours truly to thread new line through the pullies, and connect to the cast iron rack ends which in turn held the wooden slats.

The kitchen had many other good moments in store for me and was truly the heart of our home.

On washing days Mum sometimes requested me to come and feed the washed clothes through the old Mangle, this was situated in the outhouse in the back garden. One time when holding the garment close to the rollers and Mum turning the handle, I felt my fingers being pulled in and crushed, of course I yelled out and Mum reversed the rollers, immediately releasing my flattened digits, with my fingers throbbing, I soon learned to concentrate on the job.

Our back garden was like a battleground at one stage in my childhood with plenty of space for many unusual antics. Around November 5, Bill and I would get a handful of bangers – fireworks – after placing the bangers underground, just below the surface, we would set up a scene of toy soldiers on the patch of earth in the back garden. Then the bangers would be lit, we quickly lay down to get a more stimulating perspective at a safe distance of course, to watch the soldiers being blown up with the explosions. Sometimes a soldier would blow over the fence to next door.

When there were no fireworks available I invented a way of simulating the same affect by tying a long string to a stone and burying it under about 3 inches of earth, once again set the scene of soldiers, then with a quick yank on the string the stone came flying out of the earth with the soldiers going everywhere. The first time the stone hit me on my shoulder from then I used longer string and sometimes put it around the post to the clothes line, I found this also intensified the force without me being where the stone ended up. It was the same affect with no bang but almost as much fun.

The fun was often interrupted by some nasty event or another. I was told I had to go to the dentist and Marg bribed me with a promise of three half-crowns or seven shillings and six pence if I went, so I succumbed to this friendly but quite frankly, necessary blackmail. Not without penalty I might add, this was the second time I was to be subjected to the dreaded smelly gas and rubber mask treatment. This time as the gas was taking affect, I was falling into a red, green and blue tunnel of swirling lights a little like a migraine. Unlike the previous experience, I was knocked out completely, but was sick in the middle of it all while unconscious. On a good note I got my three half-crowns and bought a long awaited, double edged, leather handled, sheath knife. I always desired shiny, sharp implements, tools or even weapons.

Chapter 3

Good Fun and Naughtiness

The devil got into us one day when Bill and I sat beneath the kitchen table with a box of matches. We gathered scraps of paper and cardboard, I was about 8 but I think Bill was the biggest firebug at around 6½. I'm sure Bill struck the first match and the mini bonfire was alight, of course we didn't allow for the lino! Once it was hot it became highly inflammable and our little fire was now out of control. We fled the scene. As luck would have it Mum came in and put the blaze out. Poor Dad now had the task of covering the chard floorboards with a small sheet of tin, we probably both got thick ears for our troubles.

When I was about 9 maybe 10 I saw a £5 note on a chair in our sitting room and regretfully I pinched it and went out with Johnny Hebert. We decided to catch a bus to Camberwell Green, London, where we arrived to have a really good shopping spree. Apart from what I bought Johnny, I bought myself a magnifying torch, lots of sweets and fireworks. After spending what seemed like a terrific amount of money and having lots of carefree fun, we went back to the playing fields in Rosendale Road near the Turney Road junction, and let off the fireworks. Time to go home all too soon.

I never thought for one second that I would get caught until I came through the back door at home, a wave of fear spread through my whole body with extremely good cause. Mum, Lesley and someone else was waiting for me in the kitchen.

"Martin turn out your pockets," Mum said to me with a stern look on her face, which masked an almost half-smile radiating from her eyes. So I did as she told me and there was £3.10s left after all that stuff we had bought. I can't believe it. I didn't know at the time I took the money, that it was Lesley's first month's salary. I had a good scolding and had to pay it back by losing my pocket money for I don't know how long. This was a good lesson learnt and I don't think I stole again. I felt thoroughly ashamed of myself for a long time after, especially as Lesley would often come to my rescue in many ways. In those days a five pound note was much larger with plain black ink printed on thin white paper.

If my shoes got too worn out to wear to school, Mum would say, "Martin go up to Lesley's bedroom and borrow her sandals." So I had to walk to school in my sister's sandals in the morning and when I got home I would have to get her sandals back before she came home from work after Mum carefully buffed them up a little. Lesley commented to me once about how she didn't understand why her sandals were wearing out so quickly!

Mum sometimes used to shape a piece of cardboard to fit in my holey shoe soles, which would last one day only but if it rained it was worse as the cardboard would get soggy and wear out quicker letting my feet get wet for the rest of the day, however long that may be. One day while thinking that linoleum (or lino) was a longer lasting and shape able material, as people walked on it all the time, I had the bright idea of using that instead of card. This worked for a few days, especially on days when it was wet underfoot, being that lino is waterproof! Then the dreaded holes reappeared and it would have to be replaced with more lino.

Uncle Ken would repair my shoes using old car tyres and when I was running and jumping around, I felt invincible! I could do anything in those shoes. Some of my friends were quite jealous of them but I did need very strong shoes with the kind of things I got up to in the streets and bomb sites.

Our Dad with Bill and Martin in our back garden

It must have been around this age while wearing short trousers and braces, that after we had had chips for supper, I was getting ready for bed in the kitchen, as we often did. When removing my braces, I caught them over the handle of the chip pan and pulled the hot fat all over my back. Mum, quick as lightning grabbed a bag of flour and broke it over my head, covering me in flour which soaked up and cooled the fat. I had a red back for a while but no scaring thanks to my Mum again.

Marg informed of a time when I went to West Norwood to a second hand shop and purchased some old books then went home and gave them to Bill as a present saying, "Look Bill there are words in them!"

I knew he could read whereas I, even though eighteen months older, couldn't. For some reason this event escapes me.

One of our haunts was the old bombed out bank on the corner of Croxted and Park Hall Roads. I climbed onto an old tin roof on this site, when I jumped off I caught the crutch of my shorts on a jagged edge. I ended up with a khaki drill skirt, now I had to walk all the way home trying not to let anyone see my underpants, very embarrassing indeed. My sisters and Mum laughed so much and me being me, made a show out of it, always the clown of the family.

Bill and Martin having a pretend fight

Family get togethers were exciting especially Christmas which was a magical time for us as Lesley would always make up Christmas stockings. When I was young I really thought it was Father Christmas delivering them until Bill and I pretended to be asleep and realized then that it was my sisters putting them on our beds. I can still imagine the heavy weight of them on my feet and the crackle of the wrapping paper as it was laid gently across the bottom of my bed. It was still very exciting and we couldn't wait until the morning to open them.

One wonderful time was when I was about 9 years old and every Sunday evening we gathered as a family and would sit down and wait for the Light Programme on the wireless to play 'Journey into Space' by Charles Chiltern. With a nice coal fire blazing away in the fire grate, crackling and spitting occasionally, a spark would jump out and land on the rug, whoever was the nearest rushed to the scene and snuffed it out, Dad in one chair, Mum in another, sometimes Marg,

Dennis, Jane, and Lesley scattered all around the room, Bill and I lying on the floor all listening intently, and being so close to the fire sometimes I would have bare legs and the heat made them red and mottled. I always loved it when the whole family were together, it felt so right.

At times I may be playing with my Meccano making some weird contraption, a crane or even influenced by the story on the wireless, a space craft of some kind. Those certainly were the days. As a family in the early days we had lots of fun like when we used an old sliding leaf dining table which opened up and left a large hole in the middle. We would throw a blanket over the top and take it in turns to sit on the blanket over the hole until my sisters let go of the blanket I would fall through the hole that was another good game.

I got the weight training bug from a primary school friend, Victor Gunn whose brothers had some rusty old weights and Vic and I would mess around with them at 9 or 10 years old. I was incredibly fascinated with these cast-iron weights. Vic's brothers went on to run their own butcher's shop in Norwood Road opposite Chatsworth Way up until about five years ago.

Lesley started taking me to Saturday morning pictures, which I really enjoyed and continued to for quite a few years and by then with me taking my brother Bill. I even got my sixpenny admission paid by Mrs Lodge if I took her son Alex, who lived down the road, to protect him from yobs as he was a shy, skinny boy. I seemed to always be defending and protecting boys and girls in the neighbourhood, although I wasn't a fighter but I detested bullies from a very early age and always stood up to them. I was never pushed around out of or at school, I think my well developed, muscular physique helped.

For at least sixteen years of my life we used to have the most severe fog in the winter, sometimes having what they called pea souper's, so named because of the mist being yellow in colour. Many people developed bronchitis and died due to this pollution mainly caused by coal fires and steam engines it had an effect on my throat as well. One year in particular Lesley took me across the road outside our house, by a pillar box and turned me around, then disappeared back across the road. I didn't know where I was, the fog was so thick and I could barely see my hand in front of my face one or other of my sisters would always be doing something involving Bill or I, it might be going somewhere or listening to a piece of music. I recollect very clearly one of them buying me an LP record of Holst's Planets Suite conducted by Sir Malcolm Sergeant. The whole family sat in the kitchen again while we listened to it, I have a passion for this style of music. Unfortunately while sitting on an armchair, Lesley inadvertently sat on the record which was left there and buckled it so it never sounded the same again.

Left: Martin in the kitchen listening to the wireless
Right: Martin deep in thought at the old kitchen table
Sketched by my sister Jane, the Artist

I was bought a violin for a birthday, as my sisters were
continuously playing the old classics, Beethoven, Bach,
Mozart, etc. and I learnt to enjoy them all. I did learn some
pieces by ear as I couldn't read music but from here on I could
pick out most melodies on the piano. Later I tried the mouth
organ, trumpet and accordion. I found it extremely stimulating
and amazing how the human brain can organise and interpret
how, for instance, each note is found on a trumpet with only
three valves. On top of that the ability to change an octave, by
the tightness of your lips on the mouthpiece. Also to master
the violin, without frets, to play any note, each finger would
have to be placed precisely to find every note.

It wasn't all sitting around, sometimes things had to be done
and there was always a surprise around the corner. Dad found

water flooding into the lounge room one day. There was a burst lead water pipe running up inside the shutter casing by the lounge room window at 108 Rosendale Road. I watched with great interest, my Dad, who wasn't a plumber repairing the burst by hammering the split shut and applying paint to the area, then binding layer after layer of rag and paint and leaving it to dry before turning on the water again. That repair was still holding to my knowledge when I was working at age sixteen. It was around this time when Dad was doing something in the lounge, I was with him and there was a big rat sitting washing itself on the back of the armchair, as quick as lightning Dad threw his hammer and hit it on the head killing it stone dead. I can still smell that rat when I think about it.

Sometimes I would cause a little damage as well. I shamefully used to put the poker in the sitting room fire until it was white hot and pushing it through the floor boards and skirtings. It was fascinating watching a small ring of flames licking around the poker, and a big puff of smoke forcing its way past the now cooling poker until sadly the poker lost its heat and back in the fire it went. As you can imagine I was told off and it was carefully explained how it could burn the house down. So next time I would lift the carpet so the new holes I was about to make were hidden, also a cup of water standing by to throw over the hole when finished. Who would have boys if they knew what I know.

Chapter 4

Climbing for the View

Attempt something you think would be beyond your
capability,
you will be amazed at your achievements.

MB

It's true, boys have their uses, Mum was always asking me
to take a look at one thing or another to fix it. One time she
asked me to check our old Ferranti wireless set which worked
on battery power with glass valves. I proceeded to remove,
clean and replace parts and after some time switched it on, lo
and behold it worked! I must admit I don't to this day know
how. Another time Mum asked me to take the element out of
the electric iron and go across the road to Carlin & Horne, an
electrical shop to get a new element to fit. Of course I did and
it worked. I was subsequently proud of myself as I was only
nine or ten. If I hadn't had this sort of encouragement at my
early developmental stage, I know I definitely would not have
achieved the satisfaction in my life that I have.

"Do not train a child to learn by force or harshness; but direct them to it by what amuses their minds, so that you may be better able to discover with accuracy the peculiar bent of the genius of each."

Plato

'What goes around comes around' as the saying goes, is realized when after doing enjoyable but necessary jobs for Mum, Dad would come home from work and sometimes he would come into the garden where Bill and I were playing, call us to him, ask us which hand, with his hands behind his back, and a big smile on his face then we would choose. One time in particular we got colourful North American Indian wooden canoes, about six inches long with oars and a plastic Indian sitting in it. Also a bag of sports gums, sweets shaped like footballs, tennis rackets, hockey sticks and lots of other sporty items. I can still see him to this day standing there with that terrific smile on his face whenever he greeted us.

More surprises were in store for us at Christmas which was always a fun time at home with my parents and siblings. We made paper chains the old fashioned way, all of us getting stuck into decorating our big living room, climbing on the backs of armchairs, even on the beautiful marble mantelpiece over the equally beautiful fireplace.

Also there was the shopping in Brixton Market for fruit, veggies and nuts with Marg and Jane, it was always enjoyable, even though I was the donkey. I never minded carrying as it was all exercise to me and I needed lots of it with the energy I had as a child.

Cleaning the windows of our house was another mammoth task. I would start at the top floor and work down. Sitting on the outside window sill I would shuffle the two sashes up and down to clean where they overlapped. Sometimes one of my sisters would hold my legs while doing the top floors. I never seemed to be afraid of heights or hard physical exercise.

While on the subject of exercise and heights, once Johnny Hiberd and I decided to climb the Crystal Palace TV Transmitter Tower which was situated in the Crystal Palace Grounds and stood 718 feet high (219 metres) and could be seen for miles. The first twenty odd feet were the worst, as there wasn't a built in ladder. Johnny got about three quarters of the way up and I almost made it to the top. As the wind was fairly strong that day and would blow the tower about two or three feet in any direction it was very scary, so we very carefully returned to earth, the view was fantastic though I could see all over London.

> *"You can discover more about a person in an hour of play than in a year of conversation."*
>
> *plato*

Crystal Palace Transmitter

View of Crystal Palace TV transmission tower, which I climbed

Another stunt involved deciding to test out an umbrella as a parachute. So out to the garden again to the outhouse building, which was attached to the house, where a copper and mangle were used. Up on to the roof I climbed, it was probably about 7 feet high rising to 9 feet at the ridge, I stood at around 8 feet high, took a breath and jumped. Well of course the umbrella turned inside out and I landed crumpled in a heap on the ground, nursed my pain for a few minutes and started to think of something else to occupy my time.

After seeing the film 'The Dam Busters', while the thought was still in my mind, I went down the garden and dug two holes side by side and roughly 18" x 12" with undisturbed ground in between of about 3" wide. Next I would fill one hole with water which soon made the section in the middle – my dam – gradually collapse allowing water to push through to the other reservoir, with a little help from me, throwing stones at my dam. I wish I had a camcorder in those days, even a camera to have a photographic record of all my missions and adventures, of course I would have had to have the foresight and discipline as well, one can only dream.

I often had vivid dreams and would quite often dream I was flying. One dream in particular – I was aged about ten – was where I flew out of the window, which I had open all year round, and across the trees, over roads and a park with a big paddling pool. Later, I discovered it looked like Norwood Park. Many years later, in fact, after I found my natural family, I picked up a map of the areas around Norwood and Dulwich and drew an 'as the crow flies' line from 108 Rosendale to Norwood Park to see where it ended up. It crossed the paddling pool in the park and over the top end of Highfield Hill which I know was the street where my birth mother lived, at number six, when she was pregnant with me. Coincidence of course but nevertheless it was spooky.

Back to my missions, sometimes while knocking around the streets – once with Michael Vesty – we walked up South Croxted Road, heading towards the Paxton roundabout, with a fence on our left, just asking to be climbed. We were near the place for scrumping apples, as there was a big garden with an orchard, we would climb the forbidding fence and pick about six apples each. One of us would climb back over when done, while the other passed these big juicy apples over or through, if there was a hole in the fence. We would then put the apples in our jumpers or coats, eating one on our way home.

Once we were collared by the local bobby (policeman) on his beat, who gave us a good talking to about trespassing and thumped us around the heads with his proverbial cape while saying 'don't let me catch you two again or I will nick you.' Go home was his next order just before he turned and strode off munching on one of our apples!

The Paxton roundabout and the nearby green, which runs along the side of Gipsy Hill, was used as a burial site for thousands of plague victims in the days of the black death.

Chapter 5

Neighbours and the Garden

Next door to us at 110 lived an old man, Jim Gowler, who
became a good friend over my first 16 years until his death
at a ripe old age of 87. He was a retired City of London
policeman and would make funny noises, then duck down
behind the fence, which was about four and a half feet high.
After a few times of playing this game, sometimes, he would
hand me something to eat. Once he handed me a fruit pie with
evaporated milk on it, that his daughter had prepared for him
and he didn't want, the milk had soaked into the pie where
it had been standing for who knows how long but it was still
good. He would also give me tips like using a certain plant
sap he would put on mouth ulcers and said it would heal them.
When I was a little older, around fourteen or fifteen, he called
me to the fence, checked that nobody was watching, then he
handed me a glass of his home made cider or marrow wine.
I watched how he made the cider in an old wooden barrel
where he would put a few gallons of water and baskets of his
windfall apples plus at least two bags of sugar, stir it, cover it
and leave it. After a couple of weeks he would call me to the
fence and lift the cover off the barrel where there was thick
mould on top. I thought he was going to skim it off but instead
he said just stir it all in until the next time, it was very strong

cider. I was never ill after drinking it, he must have known what he was doing.

Our neighbours on the right hand side were, on the top floor, Avril, a pretty girl who lived with her Mum and Dad and was the cousin of Bobby Pemberton, who was on the middle floor with his Mum and Dad. They were about eight years older than me. Bobby's Mum was quite nice to me sometimes, then another day she would try to scare me, by pointing to her window where I could see a small red light, she told me it was her dragon. In actual fact it was her electric iron which I found out later. Avril had a cousin, Colin, who used to come around to see her and would always talk to me. On the ground floor was Mr and Mrs Prested both were very short people in their late seventies, Mr Prested used to shuffle down the garden path looking at me over the top of his ill-fitting spectacles. One day Mr Prested asked me if I would like five gooseberry bushes. I agreed and planted them next to the apple tree, after about a year I had my first harvest. One year when there were so many that Mum made lots of gooseberry jam and it was so nice. I still look for a good gooseberry jam while shopping.

Mum would quite often ask me to go shopping and for a while she gave me the Ration Books, as for some time after the war some foods were still rationed. Most of the time I went across the road as there were fourteen odd shops of all kinds, and occasionally I ventured up to the shop next door to the barber, which was a tiny sweet shop called Carters. The old man there used to make up his own bottles of drink, known to us as penny drinks, he had two different colours bright red and green but both tasted the same basically sugar water. The sweets were Blackjacks, one farthing each, Pianos, two for a penny, gob stoppers, Liquorice Wood and Tiger Nuts. These two buildings are still there today. Then I discovered you didn't have to buy all your food, sometimes you could make it yourself, as Mum pointed out when a bottle of milk had gone solid and said to me,

"Throw that bottle of cheese out please Martin."

I replied, "Can I actually make some cheese with it?"

I knew she meant the bottle of milk and I asked her how to do it. She went out of the room and came back with a stocking and said,

"Put the sour milk in the stocking and hang it up for at least two weeks."

I did as she had said. After a couple of weeks I was amazed at the way it had reduced from a pint to about half a cup of beautiful cream cheese. After Mum had explained that it should be seasoned with some salt and a little pepper, I ate it with some bread and butter. It was so nice. Lesley used to make some delicious dishes, she would cook things like cheese scones and I loved her cheese straws. She was such a good cook, Shrewsbury biscuits was another favourite. One of my favourite foods although very naughty was bread and dripping with salt

Speaking of Lesley, she and one of her friends, Pat Granados, who lived in Idmiston Road, took me to the Rookery in Brockwell Park for a walk around. I was about 12 and it had been raining, there were puddles everywhere. Lesley dared me to stand on my head in the middle of a large muddy puddle, so me being me I did just that. I always loved to make people laugh and still do.

One winter at Rosendale Road, it had snowed heavily and Lesley urged me to get into my swimming trunks, go into the back garden and roll around in the thick snow, which again I did and it was extremely exhilarating. I thought at that moment that if you mean to do something then just do it, this way you can overcome any fear of pain, cold or any other sensory discomfort. Nowadays I recognise this as having focus and mind over matter.

It seems incredible to me now but when I was a small boy, the dustman had a horse and cart to collect our rubbish, they also had a spare horse tied to the back of his cart for when the other horse got tired. A greengrocer named Burgess had a horse and cart also, which was still going when I was working, so I must have been around ten years older then.

Uncle Alec used to take me to his house on a Saturday or Sunday at 208 Milkwood Road, Herne Hill I would watch, from the window in his small bedsit room, steam engines in the sidings shunting goods and passenger carriages back and forth. Some of the trains were as close as forty feet from the window as the back yard was only about twenty feet long. While I was busy train watching, Alec would be cooking duck eggs and chips on an old primus stove fuelled by paraffin oil. When I got older, after he had shown me how, he would say,

"Get the stove going my lad," and I would get the mentholated spirit, put it in the little tray below the pipes, which heat the fuel up and when hot, I would pump like mad until it sprang to life and burned with a nice blue flame.

He often took me to West Byfleet and deep in my memory is a long straight road where we would ride into a whole forest of Sweet Chestnut trees, the air was filled with an aged scent of damp leaves and bark which left me feeling I was in another time. Alec's purpose was to gather as many of these shiny brown nuts as we could, bring them home and cook them on the old kitchen range. There were stacks of sweet chestnut cases after we had finished, it was such a shame to see those lovely shiny shells all burnt from cooking, but into the rubbish bin they went.

In the old days getting rid of unwanted junk or rubbish wasn't as easy as today. Mum often asked me to dig a hole in the back garden to bury the junk, at eight, nine or ten this was music to my ears as I loved digging holes. I would jump to it and have a large hole dug within in two to three hours, but digging was often made difficult because the River Effra ran under our garden. It would get quite messy being clay. One instance where I got carried away and tried to follow the river, shoring up as I went with odd pieces of wood laying around. I had in fact tunnelled about nine feet and gone under next door's fence, the mound of earth was immense. Apparently my brother-in-law, Dennis, was sent down the garden to get me in for tea. When he saw I wasn't there he went off scouting for me. I couldn't hear him through about a metre of soil and under next door's garden! I realised some time later this must have been where I was, because I saw a point of a fence post sticking down from the roof of the tunnel which was giving me problems but I didn't know that's what it was at the time.

Years later when visiting Bill, next door, at 106 Rosendale Road around 2003, I noticed a depression in the ground where my tunnel had collapsed over the years. The thought of this was quite strange after about fifty years.

Mum was very laid back about things I got up to, she had a great sense of calm about her and seemed to have lots of faith in my abilities with anything physical or practical. I loved her dearly.

Chapter 6

All Black and White

When I lived at 108 Rosendale we used to have coal delivered and sometimes the coalman would open up a manhole by the front steps, as the coal cellar was situated below these steps with access down a chute to the coal cellar.

Other times he would open the back door and shout out,

"Coalman! 'Ow many would ya like t'day luv?"

Mum would answer then he would come through the back door and along the passage, to a door leading into the coal cellar.

I used to stand and watch as the two men covered in coal dust, carried big coal sacks with 112 lbs of coal in each, the smell was so strong but nice. On some occasions, she would have a ton (20 bags) of best coal and other times nuts – small pieces of coal – then Mum would ask if they would like a cuppa when they finished, and they would come into the kitchen and sit down, black as the ace of spades and chat for at least twenty minutes.

I used to like old Tomlinson the coalman, he would say,

"'Ow are ya today Martin?" and rub his black hand over my then blond hair, making me smell of coal too.

Having open coal fires in the old days meant we had to make our own fire lighters out of newspaper by rolling each sheet into a tube about 1 inch in diameter, then loosely tie it into a knot. Fire now set, fire lighters first, wooden sticks, then very carefully lay the coal on. If the coal was a little damp it may have needed some help to burn properly. So the trick here was to extend the poker length by putting it into the open-ended handle of the small fireside shovel and standing them vertically against middle of the fireplace arch. Then with a newspaper held tight across it, air would be forced or drawn over the fire making it blaze and roar until a good fire was achieved.

We seemed to have a great deal of people calling at 108, like the Provident Insurance man, Mike Benson and Mr Mayo. Mum would get a Provident cheque from Mike – who was a tall, dark, good looking Flash Harry type – to buy our school clothes and shoes. Also there was the man who came to empty the gas or electric meters which accepted one shilling, two shilling and I think even a half crown – two shillings and six pence – when he came and turned all the coins out on the kitchen table, we would watch to see how many steel washers there were. Dad used to keep Mum well supplied with these washers in case we had no change late at night. It was so funny, the man soon got used to us. In saying that even with all those washers we still had a fair refund as the meter was deliberately set to overcharge us. I think Mum had something to do with this and used the meter as a moneybox!

Also I used to like it when the chimney sweep would come, I always watched him and he would talk nonstop. He would start by putting a white sheet with a linen tube sewn onto it which allowed him to push the rods through, then he would prop up one side with a rod and put the flue brush with one rod attached, through the hole in the sheet, then prop up the other side. He would then push the rods up the chimney, attaching them to each other as he went. When he felt he was nearly there he would ask me to go in the garden and tell him when the brush was through the top of the chimney. He would then pull them back down taking the rods off as he went until the brush was out, then he would bag up all the soot and ask me to throw it down the bottom of the garden. After laying around for quite a time, soot was very good for the garden.

From black as coal to white as snow, when it snowed very heavily I used to love going out at night walking the streets with the snow pure white and sparkling under the streetlamps, often the wind was blowing and it fascinated me to see the different shapes created by snow drifts. On some occasions I would find people in their cars stuck in the snow, my mission was to get them out and I did most times! The drivers would give me a few shillings. We never seemed to worry about going out late at night in those days, in lots of ways it was safer.

Sometimes when all the shops were shut quite late at night, Mum would ask me to walk almost down to the end of Rosendale Road near Brockwell Park, which is nearly one mile away, where there was an Express Dairies milk machine that vended a pint carton of milk for 6d. Also the machine had chocolate flavoured milk called a Micky, it was so tasty and on a nice summer's evening it was a pleasant walk.

One summer Dad – and if my memory serves me correctly – and Tony Smith's Dad Jack built a shed down the bottom of our garden. When it was finished Bill decided to call it the old bunkhouse. Once again Uncle Ken, who worked for Marley Roofing at the time, bought a roll of roofing felt for the shed. After a little time Bill and I would sleep out there all night long which is not a thing we do much in England, but we enjoyed it so much it was like camping. One day we organised with Tony Smith to come around to us after midnight, our mission was to go scrumping as Jim Gowler next door had plums and apples ready for picking. Very naughty of us but good clean fun and tummy aches to go with it, except for Bill who had a cast iron stomach.

Chapter 7

Bicycles and Trips

Boredom can be the gateway to creativity.
If you know where to look.

MB

I'm not sure exactly which birthday it was but my sister Jane bought me a brand new bike, a Raleigh Elizabethan model, red again, a colour which would stay favourite with me into my old age. Jane apparently did a paper round for a year to buy this for me and I had a lot of fun with it, Lesley and I planned to go cycling all the way to Uncle Ken's house in St Mary Cray, Kent, where he lived with his wife Ruby, her sons Leonard, and David and daughter Margaret. Uncle Ken would make us fresh baked hot bread and lashings of butter after which indigestion would kick in. Later, my sister Margaret gave me her old bike, it was a Hercules New Yorker which was in good nick and I had many good times with it all through my mid-teens.

Bill and I sometimes ventured up to Broxholm Road, Streatham, to see our cousins Robin, Pat, Linda, and Graham. Their dad was our Dad's younger brother Ron and his wife

Nell. It was Robin who gave me his old pushbike, which was my first, when I was younger.

On many occasions Dennis, my brother-in-law, used to take me out for a couple of hours to Victoria Railway Station, where we would go into the News Theatre – sadly was demolished in 1981 – which showed nonstop cartoons and news on about an hour and a half loop. It seemed fantastic then, but it was good fun. He took me there quite a few times, it must have been around the time that Bill was away at Woolverstone Hall boarding school. Marg informed me recently that Dennis had died in 2008, although it has been a good forty odd years since I spoke to or saw him, a great sadness came over me visualising him sitting with Bill and I while reading all our comics as and when they came out each week.

I have vivid memories of the comic era with the Beano, Dennis the Menace and his dog, Gnasher, The Bash Street Kids – which reminded me of my little gang in the early days – Lord Snooty, The Dandy, with Korky the Cat and Keyhole Kate, who reminded me of a girl who sat next to me at primary school and would keep touching me! The Beezer, with The Banana Bunch, Nosey Parker and Little Mo, the Topper, with Pop, Dick and Harry and Beryl the Peril, were all favourites. Some of the things they would get up to makes me think of my own antics and adventures.

Once I collected some old iron water pipe which was laying around the garden and running it from an old one gallon paint tin placed on top of our old shed to act as a small water tank. Well-connected and secured to the side of the shed. I continued to run the pipe underground for about twenty five to thirty feet and raised a stand pipe supported on a wooden stake, with a tap connected to it, then filled the paint tin with water and tested it before inspection time. I called Mum and whoever else was in at the time and demonstrated my very first plumbing experience. Mum, in particular, seemed extremely pleased with my achievements that day which left me feeling chuffed.

Also I can't forget the old push bike I acquired – not my Hercules that Marg had given me I might add – and went about removing the tire to the rear wheel, with an axe in hand I proceeded to hack at the wheel rim making deep grooves in it like teeth on a saw. The idea was to make a kind of cutting or grinding tool by turning the wheel fast, using the peddles, I started to shape a soft house brick – known as a stock. I believe this was before the invention of the angle grinder which I would eventually use as an adult. But long before that there were many other adventures to realise when there weren't more responsible things I was obliged to do.

Responsibilities as when Sarah-Jane, Marg's daughter, was about three years old and I was twelve. Marg would ask me to pick her up from a nursery (day care) in Chancellor Grove, West Dulwich and take her in her pushchair to meet her Mum from work, at the bus stop in Norwood. I often used to take her in her pushchair around Norwood Park and push her very fast up and down the grassy slopes, she would laugh so much and I actually enjoyed it. Then it was my turn again to be taken out.

Dennis, Sarah-Jane's Dad, often took me to work with him. He was a bus conductor for London Transport and I used to sit wherever I wanted as we would go out straight from the Bus Garage at Norwood all the way to Golders Green or Sheppard's Bush. When we got back to the Bus Garage, he would take me down to the canteen and we would have something to eat and have a game of snooker, as they had a full-sized table. It was memorable fun. I also got to know some of his work mates such as Jimmy Knight.

Chapter 8

A Change Afoot

In about 1954 we all moved house, for a couple of years, to Morton House, Benton's Lane, Norwood. We lived on the middle floor at one end and Marg and Dennis lived opposite us. I met a whole new group of friends and for that couple of years I joined the Scouts at the 8th 21st South Lambeth. I loved playing a game called British Bulldog, later to be abolished as it was considered to be too dangerous. It was around this time I sat the 11 plus exam and after failing, Mum had a difficult time trying to get me into a school. She spent a lot of time trying to teach me to read by getting me to identify food cartons, tins, packets etc. Margaret also spent some time teaching me but it was a hard slog for all concerned. My friends here were Michael Shea, Patrick Hedges, Jim Knight, and Peter Hyden.

If we had a lot of snow, the slopes of Norwood Park were a splendid place for a toboggan ride from the top of the hill all the way down to the railway line. Of course there was a fence along the railway line and sometimes I had a good run down and I had to roll off before the bottom to save colliding with the iron fence. This left the sledge hurtling off towards the fence. Somebody I knew, a boy older than me whose name escapes me, but who used to work at Davis's timber yard next to Norwood Park, supplied me with metal strapping – used for tying up bundles of wood – which I tacked onto the bottom of the runners on my sledge making it considerably faster.

It was also at this time in my life where we had gang fights with a mob from another estate, particularly there was an incident when one of the 'enemy' infiltrated our lines, armed with an enormous rock, bashed me over the top of my head and caused a massive wound. Maybe this is why I failed my 11 plus?

I did really try to understand what was being taught and whilst in class, at school, I would comply with the rules and regulations, mostly, like sitting up very straight and not talking to my friends in class. Concentrating on the teacher and the blackboard, so hard, was painful and yet it was still mostly Greek to me. In retrospect, most of the time, I could only learn things that I could apply to my life. As I was a more physically inclined child, it was mainly the physical elements of what I was being taught that I learned very quickly. Thanks to my Dad, my family and the natural bent towards dexterity, I can't think of a time when I had much of a problem with making or creating anything. I seemed to have been born with a phenomenal memory for faces, body language, smells and scenarios, peoples' mannerisms are another thing that I tend to retain. I have always been and still am intensely fascinated by people.

Mum finally got me in to Gipsy Road School West Norwood. I was about twelve when for our woodwork lessons, we had to go to Salter's Hill School where the woodwork Master was Mr Snead, who I got on very well with. My first project was

a mahogany angle poised lamp and my second project was a
walnut coffee table, which I took home for Mum and is, as far
as I know, still at my sister Jane's house. When making this
table the legs kept being swapped by boys who weren't very
good at woodwork and Mr Snead would look at all the other
boy's work, and found they had stolen my work and replaced
it with their badly made parts. When it came to making the
top, I would come in to find my nicely finished table top with
hammer marks all over it. Mr Snead was very angry and
wanted the boy responsible to own up. When he did I felt very
sorry for the boy at the time, especially as he was permanently
suspended from the class. I was only there for a short time
until most of us were sent to Carnac School in Carnac Street,
West Dulwich.

Chapter 9

The Return of Adventure

When we had the opportunity to move back to 108 Rosendale we did just that, I found it to be a very interesting house to live in. It was fantastic as my adventures in the back garden and the neighbourhood, which I loved, could start all over again. One of my other fascinations was to watch the road workers. After a while they would get me to help them, at one time when they were laying a new surface outside the Rosendale Pub. They were laying fresh asphalt to the forecourt, and got me to carefully throw white gravel over the area. It was my first experience of the use of a chalk line. Two men would hold each end of the line and pull it tight then get me to pull the line and let it go with a snap! Hey presto, a white line magically appeared, it was such a thrill. Then they would get me to use a pole with a heavy weight on the end (a Punner) and I set about thumping the edge of the asphalt where the steam roller couldn't reach. I was about 9 at this time.

Tony Smith, Bill myself and the gang ventured to Dulwich Park, which was opened by Queen Victoria and was a fascinating park with a two way road all the way around and a sand track to one side for horses which frequently clopped passed. Besides the aviaries and a good cafe there was a large pond for ducks, to which we fed leftover bread, and a boating lake where we would hire a boat for an hour or two, this would fill our time and was fine exercise for us. Occasionally one of us would fall or be pushed into the water, which added to the excitement of our day. There were always plenty of squirrels waiting for people to throw them peanuts. We would climb amongst the rhododendrons, which were very old and formed a tunnel of twisted branches, some of which were close to the ground. The idea was to get all the way around without touching the ground, if you did you had to start again. Another one of my little games.

On coming home I had more crazy ideas. We often had council workman around to do work on the house, one day in particular they left a very long rope which they used with a pulley wheel to get materials up to the top of the house, which had four levels. I decided to take the rope up to my bedroom, which was on the third floor and tied it to a thick timber across my bedroom window then threw it down to ground, then I took the other end of the rope down the garden to the apple tree and tied it about three feet from the ground as tight as I could. After finding a suitable piece of branch in the garden to hang from the rope, I tested it from just above ground level, using Dad's wooden stepladder, it was slow but it worked! So upstairs I went with the branch and sat on the window sill, with my heart pounding in my chest so much I thought it would jump out, I launched off moving very fast and the feeling of exhilaration was unbelievable with my face almost smashing into the apple tree if I hadn't let go when I did, but what a buzz. I used to do a fair bit of experimenting with making up games on my own if, for some reason, my troop weren't around.

For years, right into adulthood, myself and my troop used to frequent Horniman's Museum at Forest Hill.

Frederick John Horniman, was a Victorian tea trader and philanthropist, who began collecting objects, specimens and artefacts illustrating natural history and the arts and handicrafts of various peoples of the world from around 1860. His overarching mission was to bring the world to Forest Hill and educate and enrich the lives of the local community.

http://www.horniman.ac.uk/about/museum-history

For some weird reason we used to make a beeline for the natural history section and in particular to view a pregnant rat which was opened up so as to see all her babies well preserved in formalin, or the mummified human body. It all seemed mysterious when we were young.

A long time after I had the great pleasure of taking my own children to Horniman's on many occasions.

One day a council plumber came to our house to do some work on a burst lead pipe. Harry, the plumber whose clothing reeked of Boss White – a jointing compound used for making a good seal for threaded iron pipe – had to wipe a lead joint, which entailed scraping the surface of the lead where the solder needs to stick, until it is bright and shiny. It is heated up with a blowlamp and tallow is applied as a flux. Now is the tricky bit, you need to hold the solder against the hot lead until it starts to melt, then holding a moleskin pad, you push the soft solder around to get a nice smooth finish and allow to cool. After watching the plumber, I went out to Dad's shed, found his blowlamp and a half stick of solder the plumber had left, and went about the process of wiping a joint. It worked. My second plumbing experience at around twelve.

Some days I would come home from school, get changed into my rough clothes, grab a sledge hammer and an iron spike, gather up my mates and go down to Croxted Road bomb site where about thirty Victorian houses had stood, until Hitler destroyed them with his V1 or Doodlebug. There was an old reinforced wartime bunker which was built, after these homes were flattened, for the English soldiers guarding Italian and German prisoners of war. Our mission was to break it up! So with me on the sledge hammer and one of my mates bravely holding the spike in place, we broke through the twelve inch top after a couple of hours. Over the next month or two we broke the whole top off, this was good fun and excellent exercise for us, I was always instigating these sorts of missions. We had a lot of terrific times on that particular bomb site.

> *Never discourage anyone who continually*
> *makes progress, no matter how slow.*
>
> Plato

Mum and Dad told me once about how they had to repair war damaged lathe and plaster walls using newspapers, and flour and water paste. Although everyone did this in those days, there was always the risk of silverfish being attracted to the back of the wallpaper and eating away the flour which caused the wallpaper to eventually fall off. There were many wartime stories to come.

When the V1 or Doodlebug – as it was called by the English people – landed at the back of our house, I was fascinated to hear how Marg was lifted out of her bed and simultaneously the window glass fell onto the bed. Then without a scratch, she was dropped back on top of it still fast asleep. Lesley had a narrow escape, I believe, with the same bomb when the side door blew off and came through her bedroom door and ended up by the side of her bed wedged between the floor and the wall only inches away from where her head was hanging over the side of her bed, spooky.

Jane made me a surprise thirteenth birthday cake, I can see it quite clearly even now as it had a picture painted in food colouring, on the snow white icing, of a cowboy facing front and holding two Colt 45 revolvers and below that a caption that said 'Hands up or I'll shoot!'

I thought around this age that I would like to earn my own money and be able to spend it on whatever I chose.

Chapter 10

Work, Dramas and Play

I would help Albert the milkman for a little pocket money at the weekends. He had an electrically operated handcart or float which had a handle that came out from the front axle, this had a lever which switched on the power that turned the wheels. To steer it you moved the handle from side to side. one extremely difficult week it had snowed heavily and the cart got stuck a few times, so I would push with all I had to get it out of the gutter and I did, helping Albert I learned how to carry 4 pint bottles of milk in each hand and while walking on icy pavements this seemed a big achievement at the time. Albert was a very friendly man and had a great sense of humour but I felt that he had a few worries, never-the-less he was good fun to be with. I have to laugh when I think of our previous old milkman, Ginger, who called one day and when Mum answered the door, with Bill clinging to one leg, Ginger said to Bill,

"Hello sonny how are you today?"

Bill quickly retorted with two words "shit face," because Ginger's face was covered in an enormous amount of freckles!

I couldn't wait to let off a bit of steam and I always looked forward to coming home from school and after swinging up and over the bars that braced the tall fence to the wall, I would climb up the large drain pipe at the side of our old Victorian house up to the third floor landing window where the pipe ran alongside, lean over to push the window open and crawl in. After getting into my old clothes, run downstairs to the kitchen, where Mum was most of the time and say hello, then out into the garden and shin straight up to the top of the old elm tree, which was around 3-4 feet in diameter at the base and approximately 40 feet high to the top of the main trunk. I knew every foot and hand hold like the back of my own hand but only took one hand or foot off at any one time so if a branch broke off I would be safe.

Other days I would go out on my bike that Jane bought me, one such time with Bill on the crossbar. We only went as far as the new building site just passed Elmworth Grove. At that time it was running next to the block of houses we lived in. I left my bike against a shed near the pavement and we ventured on to the site to see what was going on, when an old man came striding towards us waving his arms wildly in the air, shouted in an aggressive manner at us and shaking his fist over his head, when he grabbed Bills arm and pushed him towards the shed door. After I managed to get Bill free we ran! Our only route was across the building site but we came up against the newly dug foundation trenches, about three feet wide and quite deep for a child. So with Bill on my back I ran and jumped the trench to find more trenches further on but we did it and avoided capture again.

When I cautiously went back to get my bike it was gone, the old man who turned out to be the night watchman, had locked it in his shed. I went home and told Dad what had happened and he lead the way back to the site, where the old man was standing by his shed then Dad tore him off a strip. He retrieved my bike and I heard Dad saying to the man, that I would probably have nightmares for a week after his attack on Bill. As, right from a very early age, I was told never to hit Bill and always protect him, because he could break. He had a brittle bone condition and at that age the idea of my young brother breaking was horrific.

Then in 1957 I went to my last school (Kingsdale School, Alleyn Park Road, Southwark) my main friends there were Roger Cuthbert, Jim Blizzard, and Steve Ainsworth. I had many good times at this school and although I wasn't any good at Maths or English I did very well at Woodwork and I was asked by Mr Langley the Woodwork Master to start turning a wooden bowl on the lathe just before an open day. On the actual day I was to continue to turn and finish off the bowl using bees wax to bring it to a shine. Many of the parents came up to me and asked me questions regarding the technical side of what I was doing.

I did excel at Metalwork, Athletics, Rugby, Cricket, and Gymnastics, and was in all the school teams for my age group. When playing Rugby, I was always the hooker and half back and took many a smack in the face from our opponents in the scrums. I had Mr Brown for Phys Ed, Mr Sherlock, Mr Harries and Mr Davies for Rugby, Mr Gent for Gymnastics, Mr Langley for Woodwork, and Mr Marshall for Metalwork, they were all memorable teachers.

Mr Chalmers, for Geography, would sneak up behind talking boys and give them a hard knuckle wrap on the top of their heads and was a repetitive ear twister.

Before my long working life, at the age of around 13, Jane asked me to go with her to school where she was an art teacher. She wanted me to build a stage set for a play her students were performing. This I did and quite enjoyed the attention I received for my endeavour until a very sharp wood chisel I was using slipped and sliced the top of my finger on my left hand, I still have the scar to prove it. Jane wrapped my finger up with a bandage and I carried on with the job in hand! Excuse the pun.

While at Kingsdale School after any sporting activity, we all had to have a communal shower. Now bearing in mind we never had a shower, only a bath, at home and the only person I would strip off in front of at this age was probably my brother Bill, when getting ready for bed. So when shower time came I did everything possible to avoid it, I managed for a few weeks by wetting my hair only, hoping it would look as if I had showered. Then one dreaded day Mr Brown, our PT teacher and an ex-army PTI – Physical Training Instructor in the British Army – caught me out and made me strip off and have a shower. Very embarrassed, I cautiously undressed and jumped into the shower. I was exceedingly shy and felt tremendously uncomfortable being naked in front of my peers, or anyone else for that matter, interestingly enough I soon adapted to the situation and never worried or covered up again. Mr Brown was a tough teacher and was soon on your tail if you did not comply with his instructions. As I recollect he wasn't happy with someone one day and had the whole class lined up in the shower room after our shower, with most of us in our underwear. Firmly grasping a cricket bat in his hand, slapping it on the palm of his other hand and looking very stern, he systematically went down the line of lads tapping them on the shins with the bat. All the lads were shouting and groaning with pain as he struck them one by one, I was about the sixth down the line as the bat hit my shin! Not a sound came from my mouth, I still stood upright. After facing the front for a second, he was about to move on to the next boy but he froze and his head turned and looked back at me with a grin on his face and said "well done lad" then continued down the line tapping the shins of the rest, once again the shouting and groaning went on. It was so funny and it certainly did hurt but I wasn't going to give him the satisfaction of seeing or hearing the reaction of my pain. A small but proud moment of my school days.

Chance favours the prepared mind.
Louis Pasteur

Kingsdale School photo aged 13

I recollect I used to carry one of Mum's old Veganin tablet tubes in my pocket – at Kingsdale School – which were made of aluminium with a sealed stopper and held paracetamol pain killers. The reason being was that I would fill it with useful items e.g. a couple of paper clips, safety pins, elastic bands, drawing pins, Elastoplast's, a very small pencil, rubber and other bits. I think it must have been my Boy Scout training. My mates would sometimes come up to me and say,

"Mart 'av ya got a something or another?"

I quite often had what they wanted and other times I hadn't.

Around age twelve to thirteen after an barney with one of my sisters, I slammed out of the house, literally so hard that the glass in the back door broke and I ended up sleeping rough under a bush, out of sight, in the gardens of the estate next to our house. Another time I left home very cross and determined not to go back so I climbed up to the top of the elm tree in the back garden, bent some of the branches over to form a hammock and slept all night only to wake up in the morning with a scattering of snow on my chest! I was frozen stiff but felt a great sense of achievement. Like all boys, my early teens were burdened with disputes with my elders.

All through my life I would carry a safe mental attitude in everything I did. One day my pal Steve and I mixed up some concrete and hoisted it up to the top of the elm tree where the middle had rotted out and poured the concrete into the hollow. This made it easier to stand in the trunk and when it was dry we would take a bag of apple windfalls and hurl them from the treetop at the Caretaker of the estate adjacent to our house.

The elm tree needed trimming quite often, so axe in hand I started to cut off the dead and unwanted branches. While chopping at some branches, without a stitch on from the waist up, about twenty feet from the ground, hanging on with one hand and an axe in the other, I felt a sharp sting on my right arm which was holding the axe. When I looked, it was a wasp, then another and another, until I couldn't do anything but throw the axe to the ground and make a hasty retreat out of the tree, falling the last six to eight feet. I ran in to the kitchen, swiping off as many wasps as I could reach. Mum, now on the case, started killing the wasps on my back. Then, treating the stings with copious amounts of vinegar to neutralise the stings, she counted nineteen. When I recovered the next day, I went down to the tree armed with zip firelighters and a long stick with a nail in the end to hold the firelighter. I then lit it up and held it at the entrance of the nest and burnt them out, it was of course payback.

The strange thing was I don't think I was ever stung again until I was in my late sixties while in Australia.

You would think I was always playing and doing whatever I wanted, but there were always jobs I had to do. Among the little jobs Mum had lined up for me was to paint the downstairs lavatory, this was quite a small room but high to the ceiling as were all the rooms at 108. This horrible green, smelly paint was toxic and after I had finished I was violently sick due to lack of ventilation I think. There was a very high level, old fashioned cast iron cistern in this lavatory with a long chain, it had a powerful flush and made a lot of noise. As a small child I used to pull the chain after unlocking the door so that I could make a hasty retreat before the water came flooding down the long lead pipe. I don't know why it was so scary, sometimes in my haste it wouldn't flush so I had to try again this accentuated my fear.

As young teenagers, we were always looking for another adventure. It escapes me how we found out about this particular person whom we used to go to see every now and then. His name was Captain Fleming and he lived in Idersley Grove, off Croxted Road, an interesting man, who had what I can only describe as a museum in his house. He had very old and not so old guns, swords, cannons, masks and all manner of weaponry, sometimes he would load one of his miniature cannons with gunpowder, a musket ball and a fuse then he would ask us to stand back. The fuse was now lit, we waited for the bang and there it was! With musket ball buried into a thick block of wood which he had aimed at. Some of my mate's Mums were a bit concerned that he might not be a very nice man but we never had any problems with him.

There were lots of occasions where we would go to the Crystal Palace grounds and play on the life-size, painted, cement dinosaurs around the old lake or pond. There used to be an old maze with a wrought iron turnstile at its entrance when I was younger, these interesting objects all seem to disappear, such a pity.

Cement Dinosaurs Crystal Palace Grounds

One of my little discoveries was to place a banger – a firework – in the end of a length of pipe with one end blocked off. After lighting the banger, once the fuse was burning, I would tilt the pipe and the banger would fall right down into the pipe, then I would aim at a target and the fuse part of it would shoot out the end like a bullet and hit the target, this was always a winner for expressing my inventive mood particularly on Guy Fawkes Day.

Sometimes my mood could be towards heavy exercise. When I was really into physical training, there was an old clothes line post that still had a huge lump of concrete cast around its base lying around the garden. I discovered a different way of throwing the 'hammer', this comprised of standing with my legs apart over the post with the concrete end behind me, then bending forward gripping the post while firmly standing up very fast. With lots of power, the concrete end would be dragged from between my legs, to gain momentum, forward to my front and hurled back over my head behind me sometimes as far as 15 feet, many moments were spent with this exercise.

> *"I know not how I may seem to others, but to myself*
> *I am but a small child wandering upon the vast*
> *shores of knowledge, every now and then finding*
> *a small bright pebble to content myself with."*

Plato

Many a good time was spent with my good friend Tony Smith like the time I went with him to his house in South Croxted Road and his Dad Jack would get out his homemade ginger wine. It was so nice sitting there in the front room sipping on this delightful drink with a big raisin or two. Or we might go into the garden and dig over the soil in his Dad's chicken runs. One occasion when Jack showed me the correct way to kill a chicken, by breaking its neck over his thigh, gory but practical.

Chapter 11

Discovering Who I Am

To know who you are is to know what you are.
I may be Martin by name.
But who am I really?
I'm alive and can still sense the child within.

MB

When suffering from a raging toothache due to a large cavity
in one of my back teeth, and having had bad experiences with
dentists, I had to think of some way of avoiding the dreaded
tooth pulling sadist in the white tunic, Then I had an idea at
the age of around fourteen to carefully clean out the cavity
with a nail file and some alcohol, mix up hot wax and cotton
wool, quickly ramming it into the hole before it hardened
and biting down hard and finish by cleaning off the excess
wax. Now I had to try not to chew on that side of my mouth.
This repair held for at least two months and guess what, the
toothache went within a day, I repeated this procedure several
times. Of course eventually the tooth had to be removed.

When I was about 14 Mum arranged for a man, Mr Durack,
to come and see us with the hope that she could foster a
companion for me as my brother had gone to a boarding

school (Woolverstone Hall in Ipswich, Suffolk). After a few weeks Mr Durack came back with a boy who was more or less a year older than me. We got on very well for about a year and got up to a fair bit of mischievous behaviour until he started to steal money from Mum's purse and would lie about everything. There were so many arguments and it became too much for Mum. Lesley managed to get him into the R.A.F. and I didn't see much of him from there on but I did like him mostly. Lesley told me she went to his passing out parade and that's the last she saw of him but I still had my mates who weren't always approved of by my older siblings.

We always knew of the old disused railway and tunnel at Crystal Palace, and one day myself and a couple of mates decided to take torches and walk through the tunnel as far as we could. After about forty minutes we saw daylight and came out at a station, it turned out to be Sydenham and part of it was still being used. It seemed quite exciting at the time, however, work called me again as I needed the money.

One of the shops opposite 108 was an ironmonger that sold and delivered paraffin oil. One day I was talking to Fred Pretlove, who owned the business and he asked me if I was interested in a Saturday job and a few evenings to help him on his rounds. Of course I said yes and one time-saving trick he taught me was how to carry the cans, in particular the five gallon drums. They had handles positioned at one side of the cone shaped top and I soon learnt to carry two drums in each hand which of course meant less trips back and forth. It was heavy work but the more weight the better, as I always loved to carry heavy things. Barmy? Yes, but that's me.

After a while of doing this, Fred asked me to work some evenings. This involved filling the cans out at the back of the shop using a metal measuring jug and funnel to fill them dipping the jug into a massive 1500 gallon tank of blue oil and a smaller 1000 gallon tank containing pink oil, which was less popular. Later Fred acquired an old petrol pump which made the job a lot easier, though I always liked being busy. Fred's son John Pretlove played cricket for England.

Martin aged 14 in the back garden of 108 Rosendale Road

In the winter I would go out asking around the neighbour-hood if anyone wanted any trees cut down, I usually found that someone did and I would cut them down and into manageable logs, carry them home and chop them up for the fire to keep the family warm when we were short of coal. I fancied myself as a bit of a lumber jack, which I did do later in my working life. On one occasion I carried a very large tree trunk home on my shoulder and took it round to the kitchen window where Mum was usually standing and the look on her face was that of disbelief. I loved seeing her reaction to my escapades and showing her how strong I had become, after all there was no point in all that exercise if I couldn't put it to good use.

Around Christmas time my everlasting energy was needed yet again. When I was fourteen or fifteen, Marg and I went to the butcher in Norwood to collect a turkey we had ordered. We nearly always had twenty pounders and it had to be carried three quarters of a mile, by Shanks's Pony I might add, no cars for us back then. When we got back home we unwrapped it to find it had a nasty green area of skin at the neck, back to the butchers we went and confronted the manager and he very swiftly took it out the back, I looked out there to see him and a young lad not much older than me, cutting like fury at the neck of our turkey. Then he came rushing out to us and said,

"Where is this green you're talking about?"

Then I replied assertively, "You have just cut it off."

He denied, "I have not." he then added, "Come out and have a look!"

So I followed and he showed me this rubbish bin which was empty, so I lifted the mutton cloth on his bench and there it was, the green piece of skin wrapped inside. With a red face he gave us another turkey and we never used that butcher again to my knowledge. I don't mind honest mistakes that can't be helped. From this early age I seemed to have a loathing of anyone trying to pull one over on me or mine.

One fine day, Jim Blizzard and I decided to cycle to Red Hill Lake, which was on the way to Brighton – later to be used for rubbish infill – and go for a swim. While we were there a young boy, a little younger than us, got into trouble and was drowning so Jim and I went out to help him. Now we weren't strong swimmers but when I got to the boy I was out of my depth but managed to swim with him until I felt the bottom, I then carried him, with my head below the water, gradually getting closer to the surface and when I was out of breath Jim took over. We got him on the jetty and started to get the water out of him with what little we knew of resuscitation. After a few minutes he gave a choking cough, looked at us in puzzlement got up and started walking away he didn't say a word. By then a lady was walking towards him with a distressed look on her face and put her arm out to him we assumed it was his mother, she never said anything to us either, just turned and walked off. Jim and I looked at each other with disappointment not that we wanted a gold medal or reward just a thank you would have been sufficient, we got dried and cycled home and that was that. I think Mum and Dad would have been proud of me, sadly I didn't ever tell them.

Dad asked me to help him with tacking down some lino in the lounge when I was around 15. There was a jagged edge to the lino at the threshold, which was lifting because there were old tacks, left from the past, under it. After telling me a couple of times, he then told me impatiently, to just tack it down but I still insisted that the old tacks should be removed first. Dad said again, this time with a commanding raised voice, to just tack the lino down, but I wanted to do a good job of it and he got more impatient with me and clumped me around the head. By the time I looked up, I saw Dad disappearing down the stairs in a hurry, I assume in the event of me retaliating. In truth I never would.

Speaking of retaliation, we used to hang around the fish and chip shop opposite my home. One evening I was messing around half in the doorway and half out, with my hands on my knees and bending over while shouting to someone in the shop. Suddenly I felt a sharp pain in my backside, turned to find my friend Martin John with an air pistol in his hand, laughing his head off at my reaction. He had shot me in my tailbone! Well, I chased him all around the block several times until he couldn't run anymore, then of course I walloped him and took the gun from his hand and threw it over the fence. Fortunately we were still alright together and stayed good friends for many years later until we lost contact with each other.

A couple of my friends from West Norwood, namely Ron and Jeff Collier, suggested we went camping on a quiet beach at West Mersea Island, in Essex, for a few days, as his Mum and Dad were heading up to their holiday chalet in that area. So off we went with their boxer dog, Champ. Apart from our canine companion passing extraordinary amounts of wind all night, it was good fun. On day three we cooked our dinner on an open fire. A group of three girls joined us and after lots of flirting and I think a little snogging, it was getting dark and the girls had to go. After a long day, we turned in for the night, back to the scent of canine farts.

One morning, very early, we were woken to the rushing sound of the sea and our feet soaking wet. It was a morning of a spring tide which was coming in very fast so we paddled out of the tent and got everything on to a grassy bank about four feet above the sandy beach. By mid-morning the tide had risen over half way up the bank. Luckily it was our last day, so we dried our things and went home.

I never knew from one day to the next what may be in store for me. Some days Lesley would ask if I would like to go rambling with her and her friends Alicia and Rowena. We would go to such places as Leith Hill in Dorking. Guess who would carry all the rucksacks? I just can't help showing off and I loved it. As much as I looked forward to these times, there was always plenty of time for my own mates such as Steve and Jim who were always ready to join me and me them, in pastimes and adventures.

Once I was able to earn some money with odd jobs here and there and had an income of sorts. I purchased some weights from Watford's Sports shop in Croxted Road. The owner allowed me to pay it off weekly, although I dread to think how much it all cost, but I know I accumulated 480 pounds total in weights with one 5 foot and one 6 foot bar and two dumbbell bars. I used to have Steve, Jim and a few other mates around and we did lots of workouts in my bedroom/gym. One day Steve lost his balance and fell towards the adjoining bathroom wall with the end of a weight's bar breaking right into the lathe and plaster wall. Mum and Dad were so patient with me, considering the damage I must have caused in those days.

Some of my mates and I used to go to the Brockwell Park swimming baths or Lido as it was called, it was opened in 1933. The park itself opened to the public in 1892 and had 43 acres added in 1901 and opened in the new section in 1903.

We would muck around, sometimes looking out for girls, and got friendly with a wrestler known as Johnny (Black) Kwango who was a very interesting and happy man. Johnny was a ballet dancer in his early days and he told us his mother was a strong woman in a circus, I believe she was also a wrestler at some point in her life. Johnny would encourage us to dive off the top diving board which was quite scary at first, I think it was around ten metres high. He had a great physique and with me being a bodybuilder, we would both stand there showing off with our handstands and somersaults. I liked Johnny, he was a funny guy and at my age I found him to be an impressive personality and great character all round.

There was a good café as well where we lay around sunning ourselves occasionally with a group of girls. There was a craze at the time where the girls mixed up vinegar and olive oil then basted their beautiful bodies with this all in the name of a tan. One girl fell asleep while we were swimming and the oil had collected in between her breasts and turned her skin almost black, poor girl, she suffered for weeks.

Chapter 12

My First Full Time Job

I was 16 when I was fully employed for the first time at
C F Palmers, a surgical instrument makers. My big sister
Margaret had organised for me to start and I would be earning
£2 12s 6d for a 50 hour week and would have to clock in
and out. Imagine a single level building with two enormous
gas driven engines which drove leather belts, about 6 inches
wide, up to a main drive shaft. This ran right through the
building with pulley wheels at many places and more leather
belts coming down to lathes, drills, saws, planers and milling
machines for the making of components which were then
assembled into surgical instruments.

Quite often Alf Gardner, the maintenance man who looked
after the engines, would shout out "Martin come and help
me start the engines" which of course I would. They were
thundering machines with terrific power and had names, one
of them was something like Rosalie. I would have to push
the 4 foot diameter fly wheels as fast as I could until Alf
turned on the gas. Suddenly the fly wheel would be snatched
from my hands as the engine took over, what a great thrill.
These engines, would power at least 60 or more machines at
a time, which I worked on. For the engineer-minded readers,

machines such as the trusty Victoria milling machine, the Boxford and Myford lathes, capstan lathes, and the enormous Lancaster lathe, which is about 18 to 20 feet long with a chuck weighing in at 40 kilos or 88 pounds.

I had been warned that after about two months of joining Palmers I would have to go through an initiation ceremony. Someone gave me the tip that if my clock card was missing, this was the time it would happen, after work. So before clocking off at night I would check my card until one day it was gone, so I ran out, got on my push bike and shot up the drive as quick as I could and escaped. They tried twice and failed, then about two months later on their third attempt they succeeded. By this time I had a motorbike. A big lad, Billy Flower, was waiting outside and as I drove up the drive he put his arm out and pulled me from my bike on to my back and sat on my chest. I was winded from the fall and four other lads jumped on me and held me down while they pulled down my trousers and underpants then applied grease, iron filings and engineers marking blue ink to my genitals. I needed three baths that night and my clothes were wrecked! Marg was furious and went up to see my boss. This was a little embarrassing and I don't know what happened about it.

My first motorbike was a maroon coloured James 150cc, for £10. I bought it from a friend, Rodney Hurren, who lived in Chestnut Road, West Norwood. I learnt to ride it going up and down the back garden. One day it snowed and I couldn't resist riding it again up the back garden, which ended up looking like a ploughed field after the snow melted. Over the years I had several more motorbikes, an ex-army Royal Enfield, a Triumph and a 650cc Panther and sidecar, which I used for my business before I purchased my van. A good friend at that time, Mick Rice, helped me to do some work on the engine of the Royal Enfield. Also around this time I knocked about with John Copplestone, Paul Goodman and Eddy Bowdry. John Copplestone had a really nice red Gilera sports motorbike at the time, however one dreadful day it caught fire down by the old playing fields in Rosendale Road John tried desperately to put it out, as if his life depended on it.

All the apprentices at Palmers decided to grow beards and whoever kept their fuzz the longest would be the champion. This went on for at least six weeks until gradually one by one the competitors said goodbye to their facial hair. But not yours truly and I am still wearing my winter growth to this day, 53 years on. I am still waiting for my prize.

My first task at Palmer was to make thousands of hooks and eyes out of brass wire using two jigs, one for the hooks and the other for the eyes. It became very boring as it went on for two whole weeks. After my work was done, they had to be chrome plated. Apparently it didn't matter how many I made as it was just a case of doing two weeks. My second task was to file the edges off various castings and make them smooth after the milling process had left the edges sharp. After about 6 months of brazing, welding, turning and some electrical re-wiring of electric motors, I got to work on the heart and lung pumps, which was very interesting. The man teaching me was Bill Northall who was a tough northerner, but I liked him and we got on very well.

After a few weeks of working at Palmers, one of the apprentices, Doug Seward, came up to me and said,

"We have decided your nickname is going to be 'Muscles'."

Here I am ready for action aged about16

At Christmas that year apprentices had a Christmas tree with little presents on it. I opened mine and it was a rather nicely made miniature set of chest expanders. I wish I'd kept them.

It was pretty good here and we had the wireless going most of the day. One particular programme was 'Music While you Work', the signature tune is in my mind to this day and was quite a good motivator, except when the Anvil Chorus was played. Work would stop and the whole work force would start banging out the beat with a spanner or hammer on some metal object such as a vice or tin, even an anvil if you were working on it at the time. All the foreman and charge hands would be standing with a smirk on their faces, but could not stop the determination in the lads to finish the tune, then back to work as usual.

There was a little story bandied around, how true I do not know, that apparently some American engineers sent, what they said was 'the smallest drill bit in the world' to us. Palmer's men got together and studied this bit and sent the American drill bit back with a note which said 'no, this is the smallest.' The American's reply was 'but you have only sent our drill bit back to us!' Palmers wrote back saying 'study it carefully' which they did. What Palmers had done was to drill right through the American bit and inserted the drill bit they had used. True or not it was a great story. I left Palmers because I was fed up with being stuck inside and in one place all the time.

Also while working there I became friends with a man, Frank Nagy, who was a Hungarian weight lifting champion he asked me to join him at the National Amateur Body Building Association-NABBA-which I did and enjoyed a year with them.

Chapter 13

A Time of Great Learning

Every now and then I collected my friends Steve, Jim and sometimes the whole gang. I would take some ropes and we would catch a train from Tulse Hill, for our mission was to climb Box Hill. We got off the train and would trek across a field of cows and ford the River Mole to the foot of Box Hill. At the almost vertical face it was about 150 feet or more to the top. Then up we would go, usually me first, to tie the rope. Then the girls would go up between the boys so we could look after them. There were lots of trees to hold on to but the ground was chalk and sometimes a bit loose, so the chance of slipping was fairly regular. Sometimes if it was just Steve, Jim and I we would climb without ropes.

When we got to the top there was a cafe where we would have something to eat and drink, and spend a couple of hours there fooling around, then make tracks back down. It was all good clean fun and quite exciting.

We also used to love to go to the cinema, or the flicks as we called it then. When I started to go with my mates we only paid 9d to get in and we used to love Horror and Science Fiction films mostly, even though I used to have nightmares quite often. Steve, Jim and I used to go regularly and we would come out at about 9 pm and go straight to a fish and chip shop and eat as we walked home, which could be up to three miles. Great days.

Four or five of my mates and I decided to jump on our motorbikes and go off to Brighton at the seaside. On our arrival we spent the rest of the day swimming and playing around on the pier on arcade machines, eating hotdogs, candyfloss and ice cream and never gained an ounce! At around 9 or 10pm we made tracks home when about eight miles out of Brighton my bike blew a head gasket and one of the head bolts came out and was lost. All I could think to do at this time of night was to wack in a piece of wood which I whittled down to fit and seal the bolt hole. As it was a Saturday we all agreed to pull over and sleep under a convenient tarpaulin laying over a gravel pit in a layby. Instead of going home the next morning we planned to return to Brighton for another day of fun and games.

We would often hang around in the Bricklayers Arms pub in Carnac Street and have a few pints of brown and mild beer, sometimes Lesley would join us, which was a big thing considering our age difference of six years. My mates got on really well with Lesley, I think because she had a knack of treating people as her equal, I miss her greatly.

For three years running, myself and eight other mates, including namely Steve Ainsworth, Mick Judd, Mick Johnson, Tony Crump, Barry Neville and Alan went on the Norfolk Broads, we hired a nine berth cabin cruiser. We must have travelled hundreds of miles. Every night we would go to a different pub and tank-up on beer, sometimes we moored up on the other side of the river to the pub, I seemed to do most of the rowing. How we got back to the boat each night I don't know, I ended up doing nearly all the cooking and the rest would do all the washing up. It was terrific fun and they were a great bunch of mates to be with. I don't think there was a falling out with any of them.

Steve and I joined a youth club called the Bent Penny which was run at my old school, Carnac Street Secondary School. After a short time I became a committee member and I used to take my weights with me, in my motorbike sidecar, to use as I coached the members in weight training. As there was some gymnastics equipment we could use, I was able to coach that as well. The Youth Leader was an ex-Royal Marine, George Neville, who was a great inspiration to us and coached a small team of us in unarmed combat which was to be useful later in my life.

I decided I would like to join the Royal Marines. When I told Marg she took me up to *HMS Discovery,* which is on the River Thames where they do recruiting, but as I couldn't read and write they told me to try again after one year. Marg was always there for me whenever I needed any academic support which was very often in my early years and this I will never forget.

Consequently I got a temporary job at the Advance Laundry as a van boy, picking up and delivering laundry, usually in hampers, to all the well-known restaurants and hotels in the city of London, with my old school friend, Steve Ainsworth. It was very refreshing to be so active and out in the open air. One thing stands out in mind that I will never forget. Dennis Lowing, my driver and I, got back late one day – now bearing in mind I had never driven a car at this point – to find that the boss Wally Waring had left a note for Dennis to take the three ton lorry off the loading bay and park it around the back. I said to Dennis I would do it to save time. So I jumped into the cab, put it in gear and drove this heavy lorry down the slope and around the corner, all went well until I applied the brakes. I hadn't allowed for the very instant air brakes, or the gravel which lay all over the lorry park, so it skidded into another lorry smashing the front headlights of both vehicles. Dennis was watching and said you've gone this far you had better reverse back. I did just that but forgot the full lock I had on and reversed up hill, carefully watching in the mirrors, but not realizing the front of the lorry would side-swipe a third lorry parked next to me, ripping the side out of that one. I damaged three lorries in three minutes! The following morning I went to Wally, the boss and told him what I had done. After a good bollocking, with a slight smile on his face, he said he didn't want to see me in the driving seat again and if he did he would sack me instantly, I agreed to his terms and that was the end of that. I was well and truly warned and was good to my word but left after another couple of months, with my usual itchy feet again.

Now I was about to learn another trade with a removal company, H Day and Son, whose shopfront was in Norwood Road, West Norwood with the yard running all the way from Chestnut Road to Chatsworth Way, parallel with Norwood Road. This was where all the vans were kept overnight, also the storage facilities were there.

This was where Mum and Dad had to stay when their top floor accommodation in Dalton Street, just across the road, was burnt out by incendiary bombs during the Second World War.

Ernie Dudley and I were porters and Fred Sleight was our driver. Fred was a single man of about fifty who loved his gallon of beer every night after work, sometimes I would meet him in the Bricklayers Arms, West Dulwich. A softly spoken gentleman and occasionally funny but mainly serious, I can still picture him talking to my sister Lesley, as she would frequent the pub. Fred and I would stay friends for years after I left Days. Ernie on the other hand was the image of Norman Wisdom and was a real comedian, always joking and a friendly man, both wore the proverbial cheese-cutter caps at work.

The next driver I worked with was Bill Gill, Gilly, who was a tall, thin man with no teeth and a wasted face. Nobody liked to work with him because he was aggressive but luckily I got his measure after a few weeks and quite liked him, a real character. One day we were sent on a journey to Gloucestershire where it was snowing heavily. We left the yard at 7:30am, loaded up the seven ton van, had lunch and then set off to Gloucestershire. By the time we got there it was dinner time. After dinner and a walk around the town in the then quite deep snow, we climbed into the back of the van on our mattresses and slept until 7:30 the next morning. We continued on to the off-loading address, which was close, delivered the furniture and headed back to Norwood.

After a month or two working with Bill, the tractor and trailer team needed another man – the tractor was a very powerful Commer truck with a six seater cab which pulled a ten ton trailer – and I was asked to join them as they had most of the bigger removals. This team was led by driver John Kelly, a tiny Irishman with a balding head, brothers Tony and Terry Smith, Terry Simpson and myself. The team needed four men to man-handle the trailer, which was good for getting into awkward places. We would, on occasions, be given the job of taking all old and unwanted furniture to the Red Hill rubbish tip, for this we had an open trailer again pulled by the tractor. Some Saturdays I would be asked to go with a van driver, Pete, to move usually four to five pianos in one morning. These might come from storage or from house to house. Pete was a very strong and likable person but prone to getting drunk. One day he came in to work with bruises on his face after he had an altercation with four policeman, three of which he put into hospital.

I'm now reminded of one job that Pete and I were nearing the end of, when the client asked us to throw away all the almost finished bottles of alcohol – which he had selected and stood in the corner of the lounge – and said,

"I'm going now, please lock up and I will see you tomorrow at the other end."

As this job had an overnight stop offloading the following day, this left us free to take our time after seeing the client off. Pete started to empty all the bottles into one. Whisky, brandy, rum, vodka and all manner of wines, even some liqueurs. What a devil of a mix! Then he sat down against the wall and said to me something like, "Come on mate let's rest for a while and have a drink." Not thinking we would drink the whole bottle, I joined his devilish quest. We must have laughed and drunk the deadly cocktail for over an hour, down to the last quarter bottle. Pete put the cap on and said,

"Come on mate let's get cracking, we've a long journey ahead, we'll finish this tomorrow."

By then I think I would have climbed Everest or some such event, being so rat arsed. As you can see there were no hard and fast drinking and driving laws back then, but still Pete got us safely to our lodgings, how I will never know.

One morning when I arrived at the depot, Mr Taylor the yard foreman was having a go at one of the young porters who was a quiet sort of bloke. I couldn't stand it anymore, so I stepped in and told Taylor if he wants to tell someone off it is only polite to take him to one side discreetly and quietly, not to bellow at him for all and sundry to hear.

Taylor very sharply and with a bright red face shouted,

"You're sacked!"

Two words I would hear again due to my outspoken manner.

"Go up to the office and get your cards!"

This I did. The lady who had the task of terminating my employment was Vera Kimpton, sister of Marg's old friend Ruby. Days later I received a letter from H Days, it read something like, I was a little harsh with you and if you want your job back contact me, signed, Mr Taylor, but I had already found a new job with an old friend, Tom Nicolson.

Tom, who at the time was the image of a young Jack Palance the actor, was in my opinion a bit of a likeable rogue. He was well known in this area of West Dulwich and his house backed onto the local Nick. I believe Tom's Mum was bringing him and three siblings up on her own. Being the eldest, the whole weight of being the man of the house fell on Tom, he certainly had a hard beginning. Tom and I went looking for work together and found a job with Humphreys Construction Company in Peckham Rye, on a building site.

Among other jobs, I was put with three bricklayers to mix cement and carry bricks using a hod. A hod holds twelve bricks at a time and it weighs about sixty pounds full and is carried on your shoulder. In the beginning it makes your shoulder very sore, even blisters form. We worked until Tom had an argument with the ganger and we both walked off the site.

After leaving Humphreys, Tom and I started work with Tersons, a bigger construction company. The job was on a tall building in Jamaica Road, Bermondsey, about 8 storeys high when we were there and still growing. Our work involved taking wheelbarrows from the hoist and pushing them, loaded with concrete, along a line of scaffold boards then tipping it out into the shuttering. It was very dangerous and while we were there one man fell to his death. I don't believe there was any such thing as the Health and Safety Executive in those days. It was a bad year and once again I became restless so Tom and I went our separate ways.

Another old mate, Steve and I spent some time with a guy, Alan Brown, who owned an old Humber Snipe Hurst. We spent many good times frequenting cafes or other old haunts. One such place was a mobile pie shop on Battersea Bridge where we spent what little money we had left at the end of the day. Sometimes we were so skint that if we fancied an alcoholic drink, a friend of ours, another Alan, whose father was a chemist, would acquire some pure alcohol and mix it with orange juice! Other days we would stoop to the grimy depths of depravity and actually drink Old Spice after shave lotion with orange juice even though, looking back, I'm appalled with our conduct but I consoled myself with the fact it was not as bad as glue sniffing or the drugs of today as it didn't become a habit.

At 18 I met a very pretty 16 year old girl, whose name was Susan Pead. We had all the usual interests like going to the flicks, trips to Box Hill, walks in the park and parties etc., I loved her and loved being with her. Little did I know at the time, after about 18 months she was going to be my wife for fourteen years and still is the mother of my four terrific children, Sally, Helen, Maxine and Martin Lee, known as Lee. Although nothing is ever plain sailing and bringing up a family is never easy, they are all mine and I love them all, regardless of issues and I always will.

At this time, I joined Kinnear Moodie, Civil Engineers in 1963 when they were working on the Oxford Circus part of the Victoria Line underground railway in London. As I had some experience of tunnelling, on a much smaller scale granted, I became a miner and my work involved using a pneumatic drill most of the time for my twelve hour night shift. Surprised to see a mass of concrete exposed in the roof of the tunnel, I was informed we were driving this new tunnel below and older line, so our job was to cut through this before continuing with the new line.

After my shift I would walk early every morning to the nearest bus stop and would have to wait, on a park bench by the River Thames embankment, for one hour until the first No 3 bus arrived. Sometimes I would fall asleep and miss my bus, other times I would fall asleep on the bus, and miss my stop, until the bus reached its terminus at Crystal Palace. This was only one mile from my stop, so I would wait ten minutes for the driver to have his break while trying to stay awake. On arriving home it was straight into the bath, to remove all the encrusted concrete dust which had built up in my beard and hair. As you can imagine this would not work for long so after only three weeks of torture I packed in another job. It wasn't the hard work that finished me, but the very poor conditions, with bottles of cold tea sent down from the surface at break times, and the dust and grit in my sandwiches, that was not for me.

I then started work for Wyatt's on a building site near the top of Crystal Palace Parade. I was labouring, digging holes, unloading bricks and cement etc. from the lorries as they came in. We used to have competitions on who could carry the most bricks or bags of cement. Even though I had two 1cwt bags on each shoulder and had won the competition, I had to push my luck and ask the driver to put another bag across the top of my head, but the ground was slippery and two of my workmates grabbed me as my feet slipped beneath me. It's good to have trusted mates when you are showing off. I even learnt to drive a bulldozer or drott as they called it, this was great fun too.

I didn't mind in the slightest changing jobs, as a job was more than just money to me. I had a need to experience as much as I could to find the ultimate employment that suited my skills, which were ever changing. This finally transpired a few years later in having my own business which used all the skills I had acquired over many years of trying a diverse range of employment situations. I found that interviews were also an important learning curve and I developed a very sound technique. In fact I would go as far as to say that I interviewed the potential employers, which I believe came through to them as confidence rather than arrogance. I soon learned that I could land most jobs I went for if I wanted them. This is how I learned to combat my very weak literary skills in the early days and helped me to get jobs that required a greater understanding of report writing and paperwork.

Chapter 14

What's Around the Corner?

Our house was situated opposite a large block of shops between Idmiston Road and Eastmean Road, West Dulwich. The shops, starting at the corner of Idmiston Road, were Wakefield's the grocer, later to be changed to Laws,

Morgan's the butcher, Carlin and Horne electrical shop, a fish and chip shop, Marians drapers, Lucking the greengrocer, Broomfield's the bakers, Rumsey's the chemist, Dawson's the newsagents, Nex another greengrocer. Dent store an ironmonger and H Dale the boot repairer on the corner of Eastmean Road and Rosendale I had worked for both of these.

The street garden at our house had a small oak tree in front of the basement room window, next to steps leading up to the front door at the upper ground level. Sometimes I climbed out of the window and jumped in to the oak tree, and down to the front garden to get across the road to the shops, then returned using the same route. I always liked to find as many ways to get in and out of our house. To the right of these steps was a path sloping down to a set of three steps and a side yard, half way along the side of the house was what we called the back door which we used most of the time and was never locked.

The yard was about three and a half feet wide with a fence of a good eight feet high having iron bars across to the wall of the house for support. The back garden was about one hundred feet long with an elderberry tree close to the house. As you come from the side yard a brick built outhouse with a slate roof was on the left. Half way down the garden on the left was an elm tree, then the apple tree with its swing over to the right and behind that to the left was a pear tree, which was cut down when I was about six or seven by my Dad and Uncle Ken.

Our garden was more for playing than for decoration but there were times when we planted up. I would say that Bill and I were not very kind to it but I did help Dad on many occasions to dig it over and plant one thing or another. We were comfortable companions and I do wish I could talk to Dad now.

I never found out why but from an early age I had a great fear of deep water. This fear stayed with me for many years in fact, until I started sub aqua diving, now I have a healthy respect for it. I can see myself going up to Jane's bedroom, in the attic, where there was a big cupboard with a cold water storage tank inside. I would lift the cover up and peek in with a tingling up and down my spine and my hair standing on end until the tank cover was opened. There it was a massive tank full of 150 to 200 gallons of water. What I thought I might see I don't to this day know, I do know that I have a fear of being afraid and always have to confront the fear head on. Mum knew this and we often talked things through but I was never given Jane's room even though Mum was always changing rooms around in the house.

Some days one of us would come home from school or work to find we had a different bedroom. At the time we didn't know how this tiny 4' 10" lady could move all or most of the furniture from room to room but she did. She always used to say to me 'Martin nothing is impossible if you put your mind to it and really want it', and she was right.

One memory, may seem a trifle trivial was the sound every now and then that would come from the street – ring-a-ling-ding pause ring-a-ling-ding – then in an indistinguishable, almost singing voice 'any ol' lum....ber......' could be heard from half a mile away getting louder and louder. It was the rag and bone man, sometimes Mum would ask me to take some old junk out to him. Then he would come around the back of the house and see what else we had, occasionally he would spot something that we didn't want to get rid of and would put his grubby hand in his equally grubby and baggy pocket and pull out a couple of half crowns, maybe three, even a ten bob note and offer it to me, I would of course consult Mum before agreeing.

I loved motorbikes and acquired two very old frames, which I wanted to restore. One was an Armstrong Whitworth, the other one was a Sunbeam Lion. After about two years and still not managing to finish them, I had to dig a massive hole in the garden and bury them! It almost made me cry.

Because of my difficulty in reading due to my dyslexia, I started to try and read books on subjects I was very interested in, to give me more incentive. The first book I read was 'Human Biology' the 'Adventures of the Beagle' and 'The Double Helix' or 'A Matter of DNA', as I was very interested in Charles Darwin and his theory of natural selection, zoology fascinated me altogether, as matter of fact I loved science altogether.

As with most young men, I needed my own space to do things without my older siblings marshalling me. Now the time had come to take a leap and have my independence. Before I was 18, I left home and lived in one room at Tritton Road a boarding house, at the end of Rosendale Road. This wasn't such bad of place to live and it was quite peaceful at first! I was in a rear, first floor room, with a gas cooker on the landing, next to a big front room where Nancy, John and their little two years old boy Nicolas lived. Nancy was a very nice, large lady in her mid-forties and John was a very thin and quiet man. The landlady, was a reasonably nice Irish lady, when I first moved in, but things did change later on and at the same time I had a change of job, of course.

Then one day Mum, Dad and I were sitting in the kitchen at 108 having a chat as we did from time to time and Mum said to Dad,

"Will! Why don't you give Martin your tools?"

While Dad pondered upon this for a few seconds, as he rubbed his bristly jawline, I felt my eyes widen with surprise at Mums words.

I interposed and said, "No Mum I can't take Dad's tools, he may need them at some time."

Dad then turned and said with a little cough clearing his throat,

"Come with me Martin I'll sort some out for you."

So off I went to see what he had to give me. He sorted out his old leather Gladstone bag, which I had always loved the look and feel of, together with a tool box. He also gave me the black and the orange handled saws which Dad and I had used when I was about 9, to cut up the very heavy and large top sections of the hollow main trunk of the elm tree which the council had cut off and left for us for the fire. I felt very awkward and could imagine how Dad felt after all these years. Some of the tools had been given to him by his father. I must have been about 19 and he was very gracious about the whole occasion.

General Building Company was my next job as a carpenter handyman and I had to travel all over London on trains, tubes and busses with my tool bag or box. One day the boss, Bob Hodges, asked me to do a job somewhere up in London. After helping one of his men to rig a scaffold on a tall building and hang a Bosons chair from a wire bond, my job was to paint a 4 foot diameter iron chimney with black paint which was approximately 80 feet high. On the roof I was to sit in the chair and literally launch myself off the roof and when I stopped swinging around, using my feet I had to manoeuvre myself on to the chimney. A workman already up there handed me the paint and brush and said, 'that will keep you busy for the day' and left me to kick myself around the chimney painting as I went. As I needed to descend, I would have to untie the rope and lower myself down a few feet at a time. Then I would hear the foreman shout out every now and then 'need any more paint yet?' When I did he would lower another kettle full down to me and I would put the empty one on the line so he could pull it up. Not a nice job and black paint all over me, this employment was to last about six months.

Then I worked for Halse and Sons, a building site at the corner of Carnac Street and Hamilton Road, West Norwood. Employed as a labourer again, my main job was setting out precast concrete beams and laying 18x12" earthenware pots between them, after which I would have to pour 4" of concrete over the pots to form floors and the roof.

On one occasion Gary the ganger, who was a big fat bully of a man told a gang of us to throw about 2000 bricks from one area to another, while demonstrating by throwing one brick up against and hitting the wall of the house which we were working on. So there were five of us throwing bricks at this newly built wall which was knocking lumps out of it. Then I decided to get the men to carry the bricks and stack them 'neatly' exactly where we had been instructed to put them.

After about 30 minutes Gary came back and picked out John, who was 17 and a bit simple, and went about shouting at him, throwing his arms in the air, his face red with rage,

"I told you to throw them over, not stack them!"

While still holding a stack of bricks in my arms I walked over to him and said to Gary,

"Leave him alone, I told the men to stack them."

Before I could finish, he told me to shut my mouth, I lurched forward and tried to tell him again, he said,

"Go to the general foreman's office and get your cards, you're sacked!'

Then he proceeded to bully young John, I raised my eyebrows – as I do when I'm about to blow up – and dropped all the bricks in my arms on to his feet. With him screaming in pain and his face changing from red to almost purple, I went to the office, and told the General – as we called him – what had happened and he replied that he couldn't go against him. Gangers were hard to find and surprisingly he gave me an apology and two weeks wages in lieu of notice.

John's Mum came up to me about two weeks later and said that he had died in his sleep of natural causes, they said. I wondered if the incident had caused his demise, or maybe Gary had another go at him. By this time I had found suitable employment.

Bath's Buildings was my next employer and they built timber sheds of all types and sizes, which were made mainly of cedar wood cladding and all were named after towns in Canada. I was responsible for spraying and stacking the section's backs, fronts, floors etc., the stacks were sometimes twenty feet high and about eighty sections per stack. Dad told me that he had worked for them as a carpenter some years earlier. I worked alongside two other men, a rather fat Maltese chap, Angelo and a very proud Armenian, whose name was Duncan who was only about five foot two and slim. I spent one day carving a bust of Angelo out of a piece of cedar wood and kept this for many years after. We had a good rapport and used to toast our sandwiches on a fire, which burnt away happily in an old 15 gallon drum with holes punched in it. It would be going all day long burning scrap timber of which there were cart loads.

I had carved toasting sticks especially for these moments which I found to be spiritually lifting.

After consuming our sandwiches, we usually had great chunks of Madeira cake and of course another cuppa to wash it down, alas I had developed itchy feet once more and moved on, by now I felt I was on a nonstop ride.

My need to follow the trade my Dad had honed me for, was calling me so I joined T Brown and Sons as a carpenter. They were a building company based under the railway arches in Milkwood Road, Herne Hill. I learnt many skills with them and was quite happy. Some local jobs were within a few miles and we often had to push a handcart loaded with all tools and materials. There was always at least three men on these jobs, but one day there was only two of us and we came to a hill. Even as strong as I was we could not get to the top, after putting blocks under the wheels to stop it rolling back down this very steep hill, we stopped and thought about it for a while, then it dawned on me that when they cut roads up mountains they have to zigzag them. It also makes it easier if riding a pushbike uphill, you just travel further. I told my mate to hold tight and took one block out turned the cart towards the other side of the road, and pushed it across the road at an angle. It worked and was much easier but took three time as long.

Another job I was given was in city centre of London on an office block window which had been broken. Three men and I had to take the biggest wooden extension ladder, which was three sections at twenty four feet in length, which was rope operated. The foot of the ladder had to be in the middle of the road to get the correct safe angle. Guess who had to climb to the top and fix a new window pane at about fifty five feet up? Picture the scene- a massive ladder in the middle of the busy road in town, two men at the bottom, one inside the office to hand me tools, putty, and glass, me at the top of the ladder which flexed so much, it reminded me of my Crystal Palace Tower adventure.

Time for a change again, so I picked up my bag of tools, some of which were the ones Dad had kindly given me and went to a building site in Croxted Road, Southwark, where I just walked onto the site and asked the foreman carpenter if he wanted any chippies.

He replied, "Yes! When can you start?"

I of course said, "Now if you like."

"Ok." he said and took me down to a half-built house and said can you start with fitting these door frames, so it was a done deal.

From there I went on to larger jobs like cutting very big tusk Mortise and Tenon joints for the roof carcass work. It was great in the summer, shirts off with baking hot sun belting down on us, I was in my element as I loved working on heavy woodwork and the feel of a razor sharp chisel cutting through the timber and releasing the scent of pine which would permeate my nostrils. What more could a working man want.

Then one day I was given a newly qualified apprentice carpenter to work with, Ian Freeman. We got on very well and I spent the rest of my time at Southwark Council working with Ian. We laid hundreds of square metres of tongue and groove flooring also fitted out at least twenty two-storey townhouses with architraves and skirtings. When fitting facia boards we had to use 3½" screws, hundreds of thousands of them all put in with a pump or Yankee screw driver. No power screwdrivers or the like for me in those days.

Also there was a giant diesel-driven circular saw with a three foot diameter blade which I used many times and started with a crank handle, like the cars in the old days. I had a morbid thought at the time, you could cut a person in half with this.

Chapter 15

Responsibility in the Wind

On January 9, 1965 Susan and I got married and she moved into Tritton Road with me, until we could find somewhere else to live. When the landlady knew Sue was pregnant, she wanted us out of the house and was getting very unfriendly. After a short time I explained to her that we were trying to find somewhere to live but it was hard to find anywhere affordable. The landlady, made things very difficult for us. She turned off the power at night so we had to negotiate the stairs in the pitch black if we needed to go to the lavatory.

Knowing I had a starting pistol which only fired blanks, which she had seen when I first moved in and after I told her what it was, she found another way to cause trouble for us. Even though it was a couple of years later, using this knowledge, she told the police I had threatened her with a gun! Prior to this she said she would get her sons to throw us out of the house, so when there was a knock at the bedroom door one evening quite late, I thought it was her sons, Sue answered the door and two big men shoved their way passed her. Sue fell to the floor and I leapt up ready to fight them, but just before I hit one of them, he showed me his warrant.

They were CID Officers and were concerned that I had a gun and asked me to show them where it was. I did and they said to each other it looks like a gas gun, I said it's not, it's a starting pistol which I had purchased from a second hand shop next to West Norwood Railway Station. I wanted to use it to train the members of the Bent Penny Youth Club in sporting events.

They then took me to West Dulwich Police Station charged and finger printed me and then locked me in a cell for a couple of hours. This was a great shock to me as I had never been in any trouble with any authority in my life. I went to Brixton County Court and was charged and fined £20, the case hit the newspapers. The press said it was a gas gun used for driving nails into concrete, how stupid they were. It was such a small gun and I knew what I was talking about as I had used a Spitmatic and a Hilti cartridge gun which was 20 times bigger. I wish I knew then what I know now, I would have appealed the charge and got my name cleared. It was so unjust and I lost my faith in the justice system. But something wonderful was about to happen.

My first daughter, Sally, was born that year on June 28, 1965. Luckily we had managed to find somewhere else to live, 167 Gipsy Road, West Norwood. We lived on the top floor with Ron and Jackie on the middle floor and a nurse, Dorothy and her husband on the lower ground floor. There were no individual front doors separating the flats. Sometime later Dorothy moved out first, then Ron and Jackie went too. So we moved down to the middle floor and a young couple moved in to the lower ground, they were Brian and Val Turner'. Brian was in the merchant Navy for a while. One day when both families had accumulated a large pile of rubbish, I decided it was time to do what I do. You guessed it! Dig a large hole. This was to be my finest, it was twelve feet long by ten feet deep and five feet wide with two platforms of timber, for ease of access, while excavation was in progress. Time to knock out the platforms and in with the rubbish! Our neighbour asked if he could put an old iron bedstead in, I said yes so he dragged it across the garden and offered it over the low fence.

I yelled out, "Let it go."

He queried, "Don't you want to turn it around or it won't fit?" He couldn't see the bottom of the hole you see, I repeated what I had said.

He was still hesitant so with a firm commanding voice I ordered, "Just let it go, now!"

He did and he nearly fell over the fence he was leaning on because this six foot double bed frame just disappeared out of sight. He hadn't realised how deep the hole actually was.

We threw all our rubbish in and decided to chuck a gallon of paraffin oil over it and lit it up, the flames leapt out of the hole, a bit scary at first. In the meantime Val, Brian's wife, came out to see what was happening.

I turned and said, "We have struck a volcano! Quick phone the fire brigade."

She started screaming and ran to the phone, I said to Brian go and stop her, which he did. Poor Val she was so gullible.

My job around this time was working at H Dale and Son as a boot repairer and I found this an interesting change of trade. In the twelve months I spent with Fred Dale he treated me extremely well, I learnt how to make up and stitch on new leather soles, which apparently was one of the most challenging jobs. One morning at work, I became very ill. As Mum lived across the road from my work, in Cormorant Court, I went over there for my lunch every day. Mum, Dad and Marg had moved there some years prior, I told Mum I had a lot of abdominal pain, so she told me to go and lay down for a while on her bed. As it wasn't helping and was getting worse, I had to walk home to Gipsy Road which was over a mile away.

When I got home I went to bed and asked Sue to phone the doctor, she said she would call the girl who lived downstairs. Dorothy was a nurse and she agreed that Sue needed to call the doctor. When the doctor came he examined me, acute appendicitis was the diagnosis. Sue called an ambulance immediately. After the doctor had left, I felt no more pain as he had prodded and poked my abdomen. I think that must have been when my appendix had in fact burst. The ambulance arrived and took me to Mayday Hospital, Croydon, I now had the early stages of peritonitis and was in hospital for two weeks. The day after my operation I got down by the bedside and started doing press-ups as I felt better. Two days later I felt cold and a little delirious, during the night. Like a flash a big African male nurse threw open the window and lifted me from the bed while another nurse pulled the sheet from under me and laid out another clean one and I was put back to bed with no covers. Apparently I had a dangerously high temperature.

I spent my stay in an all-male ward. A few men and myself had a lot of laughs, namely Mick Fielding who had a hole drilled into his forehead to release an infection in his sinuses, Michael Plum who was ex Royal Navy, a very well-built man who came off his motorbike and had some brain damage but was still a great personality and Mr Green with a growth in his penis, he had to have it cut right down the middle to have it removed. I recall some mornings he would wake screaming in pain due to having an erection. I was discharged after about two weeks with an open wound. Two salt-water baths a day were prescribed until the wound was closed.

While in Mayday Hospital, the hospital almoner came around the ward looking for a patient to speak to a group of nurses about their experience in the hospital, I agreed to this. The next day she came to take me along to the room where the nurses were waiting, on entering I was confronted with about twenty nurses, it was quite embarrassing partly as I was in my pyjamas.

After half an hour of nurses firing questions at me there was one in particular who asked me if there was anything that made me less nervous when being made ready for my operation. I replied that as one nurse was talking to another and while sedating me said, "Who's doing Mr Bourne's op?"

The other nurse replied, "Mr McCain."

The first nurse said, "Oh, he's very good."

This made me feel I was in the best possible hands. I must add that it is my belief my illness was due to my standing at a bench for hours on end, not getting sufficient exercise – twisting or bending – I truly think the bowels need this kind of movement to stay healthy.

Sue was between 3-4 months pregnant with our second baby, when she developed a nasty chest infection. This may have been due to her worrying about me in hospital and rushing back and forth. Unfortunately she miscarried our little boy at home and the doctor left me to deal with my son's perfectly formed lifeless body. This had a profound effect on my mind and I saw life in a different light.

While living at Gipsy Road, there was a cellar in the basement with a small window, I ran power and lighting down to it. After learning the trade with H Dale I set up my own boot and shoe repairing workshop just for a little extra cash, it was a fairly fruitful little adventure and paid a few bills.

From here I worked for the Lambeth Council as a Carpenter/ Joiner on a block of flats opposite Norwood Park in Salter's Hill, Upper Norwood. I had many tasks from shuttering to frame fixing. One day the general foreman in charge of the site asked for a carpenter to go up and fix the front opening window on the tower crane, no guesses who volunteered. I climbed to the top of the 120 foot tower crane to find that it needed a new hinge on the window but the only way to do this was to climb out of the window, tie myself to the jib, with drill and screwdriver in hand while the crane driver hung on to me. Job done!

When I had finished a lot of the guys on the site cheered me. What a buzz. The general foreman gave me the rest of the day off for my effort. One of the men, Andy, who I worked with was always threatening me, in a joking way I thought, to shave my beard off. One day four men, led by Andy, said today I would go home beardless. My answer was, which of you wants the first broken arms? After two or three minutes goading me and a little tension they backed off and that's the last time I had any trouble with them. Once again I can't stand a bully and will not to this day tolerate them.

I was not to last for long with Lambeth Council, when a friendly stranger called at my home in Gipsy Road, his name was Tom Owen he had been told of my carpentry prowess by Spencer and Kent the estate agent that owned our house. And he came to ask me if I would be interested in joining the company he worked for as one of two partners. The company was R E Moate and Co based in Ravenscroft Rd, Beckenham, Kent. Their only carpenter, who was his partner (Len Spurge) had hurt his back and the carpentry work was building up.

After negotiating a good salary, I recall he said they would pay 30% more than I was currently earning and all he needed was sight of my last pay slip which I gave him. So it was agreed. It was at least 2 weeks before I met Len who was a very gentle man, as was Tom, they were both great guys and I stayed with them for about three years.

During this stint with Moates, we found another place to live through The Estate Agent who we carried out some works for, Spencer and Kent, offered us 48 Clive Road, West Dulwich.

Sue and I were surprised one day when my old friend Dave Godfrey called and asked if we would like to go to the seaside for the day, as I hadn't seen Dave for a number of years it was great to catch up again. We accepted and Sue and I with Sally as a young baby were off to Camber Sands, East Sussex for the day, this was wonderful for us as we didn't have a car at that time. Dave and I seemed to be fated to lose touch every so often, but once I found him managing Woolworths in West

Norwood, another time he was managing a shoe shop in Westow Hill, Crystal Palace.

One unfortunate day while working, I had a job to fix a toothbrush holder to the splashback over a hand basin. Having to drill through a glass-like material it was hard going, I was using an electric drill which had been given to me by Sue's cousin, Joan Pead. Little did I know that there were some wires touching the inside of the drill's metal casing. Because I did an absolutely forbidden and stupid thing and grabbed the tap for more purchase, the worst happened. I was stuck to the tap, well and truly earthed. I was shouting for help for about 8 seconds I was told. All I could think of was, this was the way I leave this earth, but my next thoughts were for Sue and our children. I could almost see their sad little faces and thought what are they going to do without me? So I pushed with every bit of strength I had and saw my hand gradually slipping over the top of the tap until my finger couldn't possibly hold on any longer. Suddenly I flew right out of the door to the bathroom and hit the balustrades of the staircase in the corridor, breaking at least three with my shoulder. I recall the house owner's father shouting to his daughter,

"Don't touch him!"

She was a nurse and wanted to help. By the time she got up to me from downstairs I was off the tap and she advised me to seek medical attention.

She said, "There can be serious side effects from such an electrocution."

I recall thinking afterwards that Sue and the children saved my life.

On a happier note I and my co-workers would congregate at our yard in Beckenham, waiting for the boss to come and open the doors to the old and not very smart storage sheds and workshop. One wintery morning in particular the lads were complaining bitterly about it being so very cold, me being me I said, "It's not cold yet!" They looked at me with scepticism in their faces, I had to prove my bold comment. On noticing the water tub with two inches of solid ice on it, I bashed it through, grasped a large piece of the ice then lifted my clothing to expose my belly and without falter slapped the ice hard on rubbing it around in a circular motion while repeating my words to my colleagues, "It's not cold!" My lesson here was to control my mind to believe what is not acceptable to you in normal circumstances. Or mind over matter.

When we were living at Clive Road one evening there was a ring at the door, it was my niece Sarah-Jane and her friend, Beverly I think, who was holding a beautiful reddish brown puppy in her arms. I took him from her and made a fuss of him for a few minutes. When I tried to give him back to her she said, "No, he's yours to keep." Well I was so taken aback and happy, it was the first dog I had owned since I was about 12 and we named him Rusty. He gave the whole family so much joy for the next nine years.

After a couple of years Helen, my second daughter, was born on May 24, 1968.

I knew I would need more money now I had two children, so I asked Len Spurge the boss, for an increase in my salary, he said he couldn't because things had been tight, so I said I must resign. He replied with a look of horror on his face,

"Oh dear, I didn't think you were going to say that, maybe in a couple of months."

I said, "No, I have a new baby and we will need to do something before then." So I left R E Moate and Co.

Chapter 16

Controlling My Own Destiny

Only with the effort we make today can we
hope to achieve a successful tomorrow

MB

Things were hard at that time but I decided to try my hand at
being self-employed and started my own business as a builder
and decorator. I might just add that I didn't have a driving
licence at the time and was working – don't laugh – from
a pushbike with a large rack over the rear wheel for a bag
of tools. I had materials delivered to my jobs which solved
one problem. On one occasion, a small job required cement
and I had to cycle three quarters of a mile with a cwt bag of
Portland cement – which I purchased at Dent's store opposite
my old childhood home – on my shoulder, swapping shoulders
half way. Most work was small maintenance jobs and my tools
were all I needed to carry most of the time. My Mum was my
first customer and she insisted that she paid me as she said you
have a family to feed, you must be hard, so I was and some
would say I still am.

I became very friendly with the water authority inspector
who was impressed by my knack of finding underground

leaks and passed my name onto house owners who needed a plumber. When working on a client's front garden, tracing a burst lead pipe underground in the pouring rain, after two or three digs with the spade there was an almighty bang, sparks flying everywhere and me thrown back on the ground. I had cut through the incoming power cable, my spade was still jumping around in its slot until finally it fell over and broke contact with the cable. I might just add that my spade was only nine inches long and the cable was only six inches beneath the surface. Afterwards I found out that the little old lady who lived there had been digging her garden regularly with a much worn out fork which had needle like prongs. Also she told me that she kept digging up strange looking bricks with DANGER embossed on them and was lining her garden borders with them! The London electricity board tried to sue me for damaging their power line, but they lost.

Business was slow but it picked up and I was soon earning more than at Moate. Then out of the blue Tom Owen of Moate came to see me about six months into my business and asked if I would give them some quotes for work as they couldn't find a suitable carpenter. My quotes were successful and this relationship was to last for about three years.

When metrication of money and measurements came in it fouled up things for me because I wasn't very good at bookwork and fell behind with my income tax payments. I had no choice but to bankrupt myself knowing I couldn't start another business for four years.

While working for myself, my best friend Tony Smith used to finish work early and come to help me with my work most week days. Then one day I purchased my first car, it was a green Austin A35 van and Tony was going to accompany me as I was a learner driver at the time. When I took my driving test, the instructor was a large man and my van was small and he kept leaning on the gear lever making it difficult to change gears. I had no alternative but to push his arm out of the way every time I changed the gears. After that I thought he would fail me for sure as I also answered a few questions wrong. He said that I had passed because of my faultless practical driving but to study the Highway Code thoroughly, thanks to Tony for his excellent training. Just before my test, I was practising my hill starts and Tony advised to just imagine my pet grasshopper in a matchbox is under the back tyre. That did it for me!

Quite a bit later while still self-employed, I took on a job with a company called Envoy, delivering potatoes. The procedure involved picking up potatoes from the depot in Leytonstone, North London and using a company van, filling up with diesel at around 5:30am, then off on a different round each day covering many miles. While it was essential to drop off the goods, it didn't mean it was possible to collect payment. Although I did return home for dinner, I then had to set out on the same rounds and try to collect money from the same customers, if they were home, until as late as 10pm! It was a hard slog, and amazingly I got nowhere after two weeks of working with them as I ended up owing them money, which was a ridiculous situation so I finished up.

I was unemployed for a while and started to collect some animals as I was very interested in zoology, this became something of a hobby for me. I needed time to gather my thoughts to try and plan my future. I gradually acquired many fish, hamsters, mice, gerbils, grass snakes, a rainbow boa,

European whip snake, green lizards, axolotl, finches and how could I forget Jimmy the crow who was given to me after he had impaled himself in a hawthorn bush and his wings needed to mend before he could fly again. I had created a menagerie. All my kids loved to come up to the little box room at the rear of the house on the first floor at 48 Clive Road, sometimes they would bring their friends up to look at all the animals.

Of course there was a lot of work in cleaning out cages, and sterilising everything, it was becoming a full time job. I went in one day to do my usual checks on their wellbeing and noticed one of the grass snakes had vanished. I hunted high and low but could not find it. Then I noticed that the other grass snake in the tank looked very fat all the way along its body. It then dawned on me he had devoured his cage buddy. I also observed droppings outside the cages and checked to see if any mice had escaped, I found they were all accounted for. I had no alternative but to set a trap.

The trap I made was a small glass fish tank which I turned upside down, used bird seed as bait and with a matchstick holding the tank up at one end, I attached a piece of fine string to it, the other end passed through the keyhole of the door into the room. I then turned out the main light, as there was permanent light coming from the fish tanks and the lizard's cage. Keeping very quiet, I waited patiently with my daughter Helen at my side, peeping through the keyhole, I could see clearly. After about ten minutes I heard a scurrying. In turn Helen and I peeped through the keyhole, and we saw a mouse working its way towards my trap. Helen was so excited at seeing what it was, a tiny field mouse boldly and cautiously foraging for his dinner. Then he was under the glass tank with his tail still sticking out, I couldn't pull yet as it would have chopped his tiny tail off. Another two minutes went by, then all of a sudden he jumped right into the middle of the tank, I didn't hesitate to pull on the string and the tank slammed down and our mouse was hopping and jumping around within. Helen and I returned to the room and we carefully put him in a spare cage with water and some food for his effort. On studying the tiny creature I spotted he had a piece out of his ear, so from then on he was known as 'Torn Ear'.

After a while, Peter, our next door but one neighbour, wanted a carpenter to help with his work, so I joined him, which was a good move as we got on very well.

It was at this time that our third daughter was born on November 9, 1971. Sue had a hot bath while heavily pregnant with Maxine, which started her labour. I ran out of the house and tried to phone a midwife armed with seven phone numbers and on the sixth I got through to ask them to hurry as she was having strong contractions. She said don't panic and she would be there within the hour. I returned home to find Sue in great pain and Maxine's head showing! I told Sue I was just going next door to Peter to phone again and tell them to get a move on! It was quite intense and a little scary. When I returned, Maxine's head was more visible! I couldn't leave Sue's side again except to wash my hands. Only minutes went by when Maxine's head was nearly out, and with a wave of adrenalin my hands almost moved by themselves to gently cradle her head, all at once her tiny body followed quickly in to my hands.

What an overwhelming experience this was.

About twenty minutes later the doorbell rang, well of course it was the midwife who I invited in and while on her way to climb the stairs, she passed me and called out, "Hello Mr Bourne has she had it yet? Put the Kettle on."

I calmly responded, "Yes she had it twenty minutes ago."

"Oh you men will have your little joke," she continued from the top of the stairs.

Thirty seconds later I heard a scream from the midwife and some excitement from the bedroom. I took her a cup of tea and said, "Here, you will need this after all your hard work delivering our Maxine." I couldn't resist a touch of sarcasm.

When Sue's Mum came round to see Maxine, I heard her whisper to Sue, "Is that right? Martin had to (big pause) see to you?" Bless her! I can still see her smile even after all these years.

Our first son was born on October 15, 1973. I watched the birth and he seemed as if he was punching his way out and looking like a rubber toy doll, until he took his first breath. It was so exciting to have a son after three girls. I had my family and we had many memorable times camping, day trips to the country or seaside with Sue's Mum, Blanche and her Dad, Harold (Son as Sue's Mum would call him). Tremendous times. I got on very well with Mr Pead or Dad as I would soon call him, Mrs Pead was harder at first but she soon accepted me, then it was Mum for her. To call your in-laws Mum or Dad in no way detracts from your own parent, it's just a word. We would go to them at 89 Romney Road for dinner on a Sunday and they would come to us the following Sunday when we weren't going out for the day. One year we all went on the Norfolk Broads for two weeks. We hired a Mark 10 Jaguar, with a driver, to take us all, four adults, three children and good old Rusty the dog.

Moored up on the river bank with afternoon tea spread out on a blanket, Sally took off exploring, when we heard one hell of a commotion coming from the long grass, Rusty started barking. As he was always following Sally, we arrived at a scene of a strange man who was trying his utmost to help Sally out of the stinging nettles that she had managed to fall into. Rusty was not having any of that, and was standing in the man's path, trying to protect her. After calling off the hound and extracting poor little Sal from the deadly vegetation, we rubbed her stings with the lifesaving dock leaf, which mostly grew next to nettles and could finally sit to have our long awaited tea.

Another event was when Helen, quite young at that time, dropped her dinky feeder dummy in the river while we had moored up at Great Yarmouth. This was the signal for about six ducks to start chasing each other furiously while the lead one held Helens dummy in its mouth, quacking as he went. Helen was in hysterics over the whole episode, said dummy was soon discarded by the ducks and retrieved by us.

On other occasions we would even sleep in my Bedford van, spending a night or two at Pevensey Bay in Surrey, or Beltinge in Kent, four adults, four kids and Rusty the Dog. Sounds like an Enid Blyton adventure, doesn't it? Dear old Rusty. We only had nine great years with him until he sadly had to be put to sleep.

Anyone who knows Bedford Dormobiles would recollect that the battery, which was housed under the floor, below the front passenger seat, covered by a panel screwed in place, was a pain to get to. So I devised a way I could put the battery on the floor, under the front seat where it was more accessible.

Off we went, all set, on our journey down south, until I went over a large bump in the road. My father in-law Harold bounced up off his seat with the battery below, he came down hard on the seat when the springs made contact with the terminals, where they soon became red hot! All the electrics in the van were lost and a raging fire broke out under Harold's seat! He had made a hasty exit, of course, and after I had stopped, the springs were suddenly released allowing all electrics to be restored, a little excitement for the day and on we journeyed.

Sometimes after coming home from work I would call out to Sue, there would be no answer, so I would search all over the house to find her, up and down stairs I climbed, but no Sue. After around five or even ten minutes I would hear a noise. Creeping up the stairs I went into the bedroom, opened the wardrobe or cupboard door and there she was, hiding from me. I recall one time I crept in so quietly that when I opened the door very quickly, she jumped out of her skin.

I used to love playing with my children in the garden, Sally was very good at acrobatics and balancing, she would stand on my shoulders with great confidence as I walked around the garden. I started off by holding her arms out to the front then tell her I was letting go slowly, then she would hold her arms down to her sides. Other times I came home from work, crept outside while they were playing in the garden, turned on the water without them seeing me and sprayed them with the hosepipe. They would scream and squeal to stop but they loved it just the same.

Now and then while venturing around the countryside with my whole family, as we did most weekends, I loved to take them through forests or woods and bore my children stiff with my knowledge of the fauna and flora all about us. I felt it to be an uplifting experience teaching them some 'down to earth' facts of our existence on the planet. I used to ask them to breathe deeply through their noses to get the full experience of the mixture of fragrances from the forest floor, especially during or soon after the rain. Cautiously we looked under rotting logs to see what creatures lived beneath, then very carefully returning it to its exact position.

I changed jobs again – what a surprise – and worked at a timber yard, Masons Timber in Railton Road, Herne Hill, as a Driver/Yard Salesman. For about eight or nine months I was cutting and selling timber and every day there would be deliveries to make. Until the day Peter, our neighbour, asked me if I would like my old job back as he was going to buy out a company called Rundles in Herne Hill. There were about seven employees and he needed a carpenter. This sounded exciting and had a good deal of potential. I, of course, agreed and started again in about the middle of 1973.

I became a little fed up when Peter kept taking me off the joinery work I was in the middle of, to go to do a plumbing job because our plumber was off sick for months. This sometimes happened a couple of times a day. One morning I went in to work and found everything felt strange when my tools – which I had used for thirty or more years – didn't feel like they belonged to me. And when I couldn't plane a simple piece of wood, I went home and cried. I didn't know what was happening to me and was afraid to go back to work, so I went to see my doctor who said I was having a nervous breakdown. He immediately put me on a short term course of Valium, with two weeks off work. Knowing what had brought this on, plus the reluctance to just quit, this then unfortunately forced me to resign from working with Peter once more. Peter's comment to me was, "I didn't think I was that difficult to work for." I reassured him that this was not the case, it was me. I have always found a change to my plans to be disturbing, I just needed time to sort myself out happily we stayed good mates. At the time I was consumed with the feeling of having lost my most important ability, my skill and dexterity.

The only way to develop the mental tools
needed to combat depression,
Is to have experienced deep depression itself.

MB

Quite some time after Uncle Alec had died, Dad's brother Uncle Ron contacted me to ask if I would pick up Alec's old Panther motorbike from Ernest Avenue, West Norwood and take it to Alec's brother who lived in Frittenden, Kent, 41 miles (66 km) away. I agreed and picked it up in my Commer van, I took it home first to try and get it going, it didn't take long before it was running and I gave it a run up to the end of Clive Road and back. Alec really looked after it. Then on a Sunday I loaded it back into the van again with Sue, my children, Sue's Mum and Dad and not forgetting Rusty. We went to Frittenden for a day out, it was the first time I had seen Alec's brother, since I was around 9, which was twenty years earlier.

Chapter 17

Changing Career

After about a month of rest I looked for another job and found Reliance Security wanted guards so I thought, what the hell, its work. My first assignment was 12 hour night shifts on a static site where I had to call in every hour to the headquarters or base and let them know that I was okay and most important to the company, all was secure. After three weeks of this I was called up to the base in Tulse Hill where Mr Moyson, the Operations Manager, asked me if I would like to become a Mobile Patrolman. I agreed to this as I was stuck in one place for twelve hours day in and day out. This new assignment meant driving back and forth to sites, letting myself in and checking the area was secure. As I had to visit thirty or more sites three times a night, it was nothing to clock up 200 miles driving and 6 miles walking every night.

On one occasion I had to take out a new guard whose name was John Baird. He was a giant of a man, six foot five tall and about twenty two stone. As the night went on, we had a call to go to Surrey Docks to investigate a reported disturbance. At a particular wharf we let ourselves in by unlocking and locking the big steel gates behind us, John had the keys. Well, there was an almighty crash from inside the warehouse, I have never seen a man as big as John run away so fast! He ran back to the gate, opened it, got in the van and locked himself in. After checking the area by myself and finding nothing but rats, I went back to the van. John opened the door, I got in and said,

"You want to be a security guard?"

He replied, still shaking, and his voice wavering, "I don't know."

We went and had a coffee to talk about it, John stayed with us for another six or seven months. The call came from our base again and Mr Moyson said that I had been promoted to Supervising Patrolman. He gave me two stripes to put on my tunic and asked me if I would be a dog handler, of course yes, was my answer. I had to go to kennels in Blackheath to pick out a police-trained Alsatian guard dog. A couple of days later I went and picked him up, his name was Rosco.

About six weeks went by and up I went again to the base, this time there were three Officers to interview me. They said I seemed more than competent with my past assignments and was doing so well that they wanted me to be the Sergeant Controller for night shifts. This was a position with a lot more responsibility and more pay, I naturally accepted.

About two months went by and I was quite comfortable with my workload when Moyson called me to his office. We had a long chat about where the company was going. It was rapidly growing and I asked why he was telling me this. He stood up from his chair and as I watched him, he came towards me with a smile and said you have been promoted again, we would like you to be the Inspector in charge of all forty guards on the night shifts! This was a noteworthy duty which carried a huge volume of responsibility but I was sure I could handle it and once more agreed. I was sent to be measured up for a new uniform and given pips for my epaulets with a lanyard for any special occasions. This was such an extraordinary day. I also asked if I was to keep my dog, he said, of course. I would be out and about more and exposed to vandals and the criminal element now, especially as we had taken on a new job of protecting the old Covent Garden Market – near the Strand in London – night and day with twelve guards on twelve hour shifts. One day I was asked to take a VIP and show him our sites. He was General Sir Victor George Balfour, out came the lanyard! This was truly a big day for me as I had been told he used to be the Queen's Equerry and I found him to be exceedingly interesting and a perfect gentleman.

I went on for a few more months with Reliance, and sadly I had a falling out with the new Chief Inspector, who was an ex Warrant Officer 1st class in the British Army. He dealt with people as though he still *was* in the Army.

From here I wanted something a little different, it all transpired that instead of being responsible for sixty men from all walks of life, I had forty five or more screaming juveniles to cope with. While working for I. L. E. A. – the Inner London Education Authority – as a school bus driver. There I met two of the men I knew from my security job, Warren Graham and Bob Dixon, who I liked and got on with very well. I had to wait a week until they could get the driving police examiner to take me for my PSV test (Public Service Vehicle). During this period I received full pay and all I did was play dominoes with the other four potential drivers. Then the police examiner took five of us out for our test in one of the buses which were fifty-two seaters, Bedford ex-army troop carriers. Only two of us got through, yes, I was one of them and an ex-police detective, Ted, whose last name escapes me.

My training here was about to start, even though this was only a stop gap job, as with four children I had to keep the nose to the grindstone and eventually get a better paid one. In the meantime this job had to do and consisted of taking school children from schools all over London to playing fields or swimming baths, then waiting for up to four hours until taking them back to school. Some drivers would sit in their buses and play cards or sleep. I decided this was a waste of life, so I got a few of the drivers together and went walking and exploring the areas. Sometimes it was countryside or it might be the suburbs of London, but wherever it was, it was more interesting than sitting around, plus it was good exercise. I still felt very unsettled as there were too many hours sitting around, this was a trifle soul destroying and I had to move on again.

So moving on again, this time the same sort of job with a difference. It was to Grove Coaches in West Norwood, picking up badly handicapped children from their homes in the mornings, then taking them to Cheyne Walk Hospital in Chelsea for treatment, returning home in the afternoons. It was an okay job for a stop gap and it paid the bills. On one trip, one passenger was a girl of around 9 who was the last drop and lived in a tower block in Roehampton, which was about twelve floors high. She lived on the top floor and her mother would normally meet us on the ground floor of the building but this time she wasn't there. Finally the guide, who was with me on the coach, went up to find the mother who was about half way down, bringing the wheelchair for her daughter, on the stairs as the lifts were out of order. I ended up carrying the helpless girl on my shoulder all the way up, while the mother was still bringing the wheelchair back up the stairs, it nearly killed me as she weighed about eight stone. Her mother was very grateful for my care and assistance.

It was during my time here that I swapped my car – a Ford 100e – for an MG Magnet with a co-worker, Robert, with whom I had become good friends.

Well you know what they say about all work and no play. Our terrific pals, Tony and Chris Smith used to invite Sue and me for dinner now and then and we would have them to our home at other times. I loved our in-depth discussions, sometimes putting the world to rights. Occasionally Tony's lodger Tom and his wife Beryl would join us when at Tony's house. One such chat was the time Tony and Chris, with other acquaintances were planning to build a raft to hold an old Ford motor car, using its engine and with two paddle wheels attached to the rear axles, instead of the original wheels.

This they did and started their adventure, months later, across the English Channel to France until they got a few miles out when things started to go wrong and they had to abandon the raft and sadly the voyage.

Thirty years later my current wife, Corrie, has now met them and she too found them to be excellent hosts and great company with many interesting stories. Chris is a fantastic person with an interesting sense of humour, she and Tony are very personable and great friends, we can discuss just about anything with them.

Chapter 18

Serious Play Time

In late 1977 I caught up with an old friend, John Belsey –
from my days at Palmers – we went for a drink together and
it transpired that he was into skin diving in a big way, he saw
I was interested and said come and give it a go. I decided that
was a worthwhile thing to do and went along out of curiosity,
this eventuated after a short time in enrolling to be trained as
a sub aqua diver. It was March 15 1978, when I was accepted
into the BSAC or British Sub Aqua Club. Once a member and
after a very thorough medical I could go out on open water
dives and this was to be one of the highlights of my life. I
sent away for a do-it-yourself kit to make my own two piece
wetsuit hood, gloves and boots. That alone was interesting
and if I recall, it cost around £20. The course consisted of one
hour theory in a classroom and two hours pool training, three
evenings a week for many years.

Over the coming months, I learnt about the necessary physics,
techniques, rules, safety and all equipment needed to become
a BSAC diver. Choosing and purchasing my equipment was
expensive but exciting, the cylinder I chose was bright yellow
and made from ½" thick aluminium with a capacity of some
105 cubic feet of air. The air in it alone weighed 8½ lbs, Chris

Martin worked in the shop and helped me choose wisely, he was also a member of our club and a very experienced diver to boot, he nicknamed my cylinder the 'dustbin' which stuck with all the members. Because of his looks and general persona Chris Martin had me thinking back to my old pal Mick Johnson who also had the same bounce in his step.

I also went on to study some specialised diving skills, such as learning how to stay alive below the water for twenty minutes using just an ABLJ or an Adjustable Buoyancy Life Jacket, by alternately breathing from the mouthpiece of the jacket and on exhalation opening the valve of a small cylinder of compressed air. The secret is to completely relax and to alternate between letting air in to the life jacket and exhaling otherwise you will start ascending from the bottom. This was mainly practised in the pool, but a lot of our training was in places like Stoney Cove, Lancashire, which was a quarry where the stone for the M1 Motorway was excavated. Over the years it had filled with rainwater and was 200 feet deep, at its deepest point. It was an excellent training facility, this included a sunken helicopter which was a good place to start our buddy breathing practice, particularly for novices as we could sit in it to relax for a minute before commencing.

Lake Peterborough was another diving place which I believe was an old brickworks belonging to the London Brick Company. Here I learnt how to safely dive under ice which I found to be fascinating as my exhaled bubbles would get trapped in pockets between the water and the ice. It was great fun removing my demand valve or mouthpiece and reclaiming the trapped air by putting my lips close to the ice and very carefully sucking the air back a few times until the oxygen had all but gone, then of course returning my mouthpiece back. One winter at Peterborough, while getting out of our wetsuits, I was surprised at the amount of steam coming from our bodies, it was unbelievable, almost like a stable of exercised horses.

From here I went on to learn night diving, low or even no visibility diving using a compass to navigate my way around, and then on to some deep rescue practice.

One exciting moment was when asked by the South London Aquatic Society to carry out an underwater survey to the Woolwich Royal Dockyards to check for leaks. The reason being it was costing the Society an awful amount of money in water usage in an attempt to keep the water level up.

These were the dry docks used for shipbuilding at nearly seven hundred feet long and were originally built in 1512 by command of Henry VIII and many famous ships were built there including Henry's flagship *Henri Grace a Dieu*. Great ships for the Royal Navy were produced there for another 250 years. In 1841 Queen Victoria launched *HMS Trafalgar*, which she christened with a bottle of wine taken from the *HMS Victory* after her return from the Battle of Trafalgar. Thirteen years after that she launched the *Royal Albert*.

I believe Charles Darwin's *Beagle* was yet another, and the last ship to be built was the *Thalia* on July 13 1869. In October 1869 the dock was closed and a lot later a concrete wall was built to seal it off from the River Thames. To this day it is stocked up with all manner of fish and open to the public for recreational fishing.

During this survey, I had to submerge about 28 feet down and weave my way around concrete pillars which were supporting a massive slab of concrete. This slab was above my head level with the surface of the water and spanned the whole width of the dock, and about ten feet out from the wall it was almost like swimming in a cave. I made my way underwater, sometimes crawling, for about eighty feet, checking the concrete wall for leaks as I proceeded. I used a rope as it wasn't prudent for more than one diver to be in this area at the same time. Rope diving is a recognised practice for these situations which was also my only communication with the surface. With some practice it became easier to communicate with the surface and visa-versa, using a set of signals or pulls on the rope.

It was quite a challenge for us to find a way to detect the leaks until I came up with a possible idea. This was to use a supply of syringes filled with a dye and by looking for cracks and crevices then squirting a little dye out close to the area. Sure enough the dye weaved its way to the leaks in a thread-like wispy pattern and disappeared into the small cracks, then I marked the area with a large wax crayon. After writing a report on my findings, I was asked by the society if I would consider being on their committee and I accepted their offer.

At one phase in my training, our club was invited to the submariners training facility, HMS Dolphin, at Gosport, Dorset. After descending in to the submarine to view all its cabins, torpedo tubes and controls, we learnt how they train submariners to surface from 100 feet underwater on one breath, in their special training tower. The positions in the club I progressed to were Dive Leader, Acting Dive Marshal to Dive Marshal.

On one occasion, one of my dive buddies, John Calver and myself made up a team of four qualified divers in all, we were asked to recover a 50 foot cabin cruiser that had sunk due to a violent storm at the west side of Putney Bridge. It had been moored up to a boom to one side of the River Thames on the south bank. One of the team, Dave Kibble our illustrious leader, designed and made up special brackets, to fasten to the keel, with large eyes on each side. These were for securing the ropes which were in turn tied to 40 gallon oil drums. We had a small window of opportunity to get these drums fixed in place each side of the vessel. The plan was that once fixed in place, the tide would come in, then when the water had settled a little, we would dive below the vessel and with spare tanks of air we would fill the oil drums with the air, and hopefully up it would come.

But it was November and the north of England had a lot of rain and unfortunately the flood gates were opened.

So before we managed to get all drums filled with air, the river was in full flood and running very fast and became too dangerous to stay under water any longer. This upset the balance of the vessel and one drum broke free – later it was determined that it was due to the keel being rotten and waterlogged causing one of the brackets to come off – it took us hours to try to contain this potentially lethal situation. Things got from bad to worse and we had to alert the River Thames Water Authority of this disaster.

Picture this, four divers in full kit on two inflatable boats, slipping and sliding over the now freezing tube sides, ice forming on them and our wet suits, tired after eight hours of being in them, night was falling. Now the sunken cruiser was momentarily breaking the surface of the water to then disappear below like a whale. We spread ourselves out took our positions each side of the area in the hope one of us could snag the loose rope and secure it back on to the boom. Then the timber monster reappeared and rose about eight or nine feet above the surface of the water like a submarine, twenty or thirty feet away from where it was sixty seconds ago. The water current was so strong and relentless we didn't know where it would surface again. It could have quite easily emerged right under one of our boats, tossing us into the river, this went on for at least two and a half hours. It was hopeless trying to fight the river at its most perilous, so we gave the okay for the dredger standing by, to ram and destroy it. Before it broke completely free from the last rope which was holding it at this point and cause chaos all the way down the river Thames, the dredger rammed it twice preventing further disasters. We were very unlucky with the tides but thankfully nobody was hurt excepting for our pride.

At some stage in our pool training, the pool had to be drained away ready to have major works carried out on it. As we had paid our fees, we were offered an alternative activity for the duration of these repairs, about four of us went for the weight training class. During the six weeks, the instructor latched on to me as he said I had a lot of potential – as you know by now weight lifting was not new to me – and proceeded to persuade me towards dead lifting. By the end of the six weeks I had achieved a deadlift of 620 lbs. Deadlifting is carried out with legs apart, then bending the knees while looking ahead and firmly gripping the bar with hands facing in opposite directions. Next straighten your back and legs until upright, locking your knees for a couple of seconds then bend forward quickly and put the bar down.

Finally the pool was completed allowing us to go back to our dive training.

At a place called Pagham near Bognor there are three Mulberry harbours, which were built as a submersible harbour during the war for loading ships, they were very big concrete platforms which could be raised and sunk by pumping air into the hollow centres. The second Mulberry was upside down in about 30 feet of water at a moderate tide. We would dive on it because there was all manner of fish and wildlife that made their homes inside. Joe Lukes and I got a bit tangled in fishing line once and spent a good twenty minutes coiling it up and putting it under a large piece of concrete so no unsuspecting diver would get caught up as we had. That was our dive over for that day, all because of a piece of fishing line.

My first deep water dive was nine miles out from Rye harbour, it was a dive of some 100 feet to *HMS Gurkha*, a First World War destroyer, this was a fascinating adventure. I was watching the fish swimming in and out of the broken portholes, when I felt something brush past my right shoulder and across my back! With limited peripheral vision due to my mask, I swung around to see the body of a large black animal coming out of a porthole, by the time I turned back I saw its head making for another porthole, it was a conger eel! What a buzz. I had always hoped I would see one but maybe not that close.

We had now run out of time and had to surface slowly, of course, or risk the chance of four extremely dangerous conditions, such as burst lung, air embolism, barotrauma pneumothorax or interstitial emphysema. As I reached the anchor line, to make my ascent, I started to choke on seawater that found its way to the back of my throat from my demand valve. This immediately gave me the desire to haul myself up the line as quick as possible. A fault in the rubber component was found later. But for my vastly experienced dive buddy Chris Martin, who grabbed my foot and pulled me back which reminded me of the specialized training in dealing with these situations, I may not be here to tell my tale. As time was running out before the need of decompression stops he helped me calm down and get my breathing regulated before surfacing.

While chatting to my sister Lesley, she ask me to get a group of divers together for rescue work on the River Thames. Lesley coxed a rowing eight for her rowing club and they required support in case of accidents. So I needed a total of six divers from my club and our three 12 foot inflatable boats, at strategic points on the river. This was to save people in the event of a collision or capsize, as there were accidents every year and the current was dangerous at points like below the bridges and at the black buoy, which was my post. This was a ten foot long by eight foot diameter tank in the middle of the river and was an extremely hazardous position for anyone in the water. The current here could hold a person underwater for a long time. This would definitely need the expertise of a fully equipped diver or two to get them up to the surface.

This was all happening in the middle of pursuing my next work adventure with Community Industry, which was a retraining scheme to help ex-offenders and low achievers by encouraging them and hopefully get them working back into society. I was taken on as a Scheme Consultant and my duties were to motivate a group of up to fifteen youths in my well-practiced trade as a carpenter and joiner. These youths were between sixteen and twenty years old.

When I first started I was introduced to Ed Bickley, who was second in charge to the manager, he took me down to the building where I would be working. It was a shell of a building with no windows, just openings in the walls, very basic. Now I was familiarised with my group of 10 boys and after a morning of chatting so we could get to know each other, I presented them with their first project. This was to build three large work benches, but we had to wait for materials i.e. timber and screws etc.

While waiting for these to arrive we drafted up some plans to work to, it was a very strange experience for me to have people who didn't know anything about the carpentry industry or what they were about to do. Every step of the way had to be planned and I took an individual approach to each trainee, mainly to find out how much they did know. Soon I felt more relaxed and comfortable with the boys and them with me. At last our materials arrived, now we could get stuck in and deal with the business of making our benches, and what magnificent benches they were, seven feet long by four feet wide with a removable well board in the middle. Every boy had to carry out each detail of every component needed to construct the benches.

Then came the time to order some more tools including woodworking machinery, circular saws, band saws and lathes. There was a pretty good budget for all this and I was in my element now and I wallowed in it, I was allowed to take the company van with my team of boys to choose and purchase whatever we needed, it was considered to be all part of the work experience we were teaching. After tools and machinery were installed with a deal of excitement all round, we planned and executed project number two which was to order materials to make four five foot wide window frames. This enabled us to create, fit and glaze them in readiness for painting.

Things were buzzing now and I couldn't seem to do anything wrong in the Management's eyes, which was an excellent place to be. But as I have learned from sometimes painful experience you're very lucky if these situations last for long. It is far better to tick along on an even keel. They then asked me if I would fulfil the position of Health and Safety Officer, of course I did as this subject has always been an important consideration in my life, whether in work or play.

One of my charges walked on two artificial legs and I had to find a way of teaching him to saw wood at the bench, but due to the lack of ankle muscles, he lost his balance and fell backwards a few times. I made a comment once without thinking and said, "If you don't lean in Clive you won't have a leg to stand on."

Clive was a nice lad and I finally taught him to stand further from the bench at a greater angle than normal to compensate for the lack of his ankle muscles which gave him more stability while pushing on the saw. Thankfully this worked. I learned this trick from the interest I took in Douglas Bader.

Everything was running like clockwork until the proverbial spanner was thrown into the mix. I was asked to take a girl into my care, my how the atmosphere changed! The discipline

I had introduced was compromised, but not for long! I had to take her to one side and spell out the rules to her as with ten boys and one girl it wasn't a good combination. Luckily she was a bit of a tomboy and understood my endeavour and we soon all got on, smooth running was once more achieved.

Two of the boys who were quite obliging helped me to create a room by building a partition at the end of this very large area, this was to double up as an office for me and a tea room for the boys. We acquired the free materials for this project from the exhibition centre at Earl's Court, London. Old panelling and timber removed from stage sets was available, all we had to do was pick it up ourselves.

There were Scheme Consultants for all trades. Ann Bingley for pottery, Alan Neilson for painting and decorating, Don for gardening and two more females for needlework and art. One day Alan came into our workshop with a rather red face and quite angry.

He said, "Could you and your team possibly do me a big favour?"

"What's the problem?" I queried.

"Come and I will show you," he replied.

After my boys promised to be on their good behaviour while I was gone, Alan took me to a church where his team were doing some painting and introduced me to the Vicar. I was shown a pile of broken plaster statue that was the young Jesus, originally about three feet high. It had been smashed into about two hundred pieces by one of Alan's boys, whose name was Donny and was a little dynamo.

The Vicar asked, "Could you put it back together?"

"Yes," I replied. "Given time."

After some time I had the statue assembled again, then came the detailed painting after filling all the cracks and missing pieces. Job finished.

I returned him to the church where the Vicar exclaimed, "It looks like He's been on His holidays."

The reason being was that I had used my artistic license and painted his hands and face a coffee colour instead of the pink that he had been.

It was about this time when I got far too friendly with one of the female staff and had a short affair with her, I'm well aware that this was wrong and have paid the price but done is done and I'm far from proud of it. But my life including all my mistakes, are most defiantly mine. After fourteen years of marriage, in my opinion there was something lacking or missing in my life and this had to be found but, unfortunately, some would say this is my failing.

All was revealed when a person handled, very badly, a rare phone call from my wife, who had phoned my work to talk to me and I wasn't there. I often ponder on what my life would have been if I had controlled my selfishness, which I accept it to be, and not succumbed to an affair with this person.

I regretted the pain and trouble it caused by putting Sue and the children through all that trauma and I missed my family. That said, I stopped seeing this person and finished my job there with Community Industry to show I would do anything to help Sue if she was prepared to give our marriage another chance. At that stage she was, until a person, who shall be nameless, repeated something to Sue on the phone – which was told to them in confidence a week earlier – and by the time they talked to Sue I had actually finished the affair, a week previously. What a mess. That was the end of my marriage and a wonderful job.

Later when I moved in to my own room, my children came to see me now and again. I missed them so much.

O, what a tangled web we weave ...

Chapter 19

Thoughts of the Future

After leaving the comfort of my home I didn't want to worry
my parents, as I felt ashamed, resulting in me spending two
nights sleeping under an old oak tree in Norwood Park. This
helped me to come to terms with my self-inflicted situation.
With this time totally on my own, I mulled it over and decided
to phone my very good friend Tony Smith and imparted my
predicament to him.

He said without any hesitation,

"Tell me where you are, I'll come and pick you up."

He then drove for three and a half hours all the way down
from Norfolk, picked me up and then took me back to his and
his wife Chris's house for a couple of weeks. They helped
me to get my head around my hopefully once in a lifetime
ordeal, – you don't get many friends like that in a lifetime.

On my return to London I spoke to Sue who told me she
needed more time and I next spent two weeks at my sister
Marg's flat in Clifftonville, Kent near Margate. My days
here were spent reflecting on my past and contemplating my

future. This involved lots of walking, and I usually packed a sandwich, drink, and apple to walk for miles in an attempt to sort out my mind.

My first walk was from Clifftonville to Pegwell Bay, a cross-country trip of seven miles each way. The next trip was to Deal, Kent which was quite exhausting, leaving at 7am until 8pm covering a distance of 18 miles (29 kms) each way. On my return to West Dulwich, I found a room in Lancaster Avenue, West Norwood and there I stayed for about eighteen months.

I became occupied and fully focused on Sub Aqua Diving. While living there and walking up to the shops in Norwood Road, I witnessed a nasty accident where an old car came down York Hill opposite Lancaster Avenue and tried to turn right into Norwood Road. The car overturned onto its side so I ran to help the elderly male driver out, while people were screaming and shouting to mind the petrol!

I had noticed it flooding to the gutter, but I couldn't bear the thought of that old man burning alive so I moved fast. I jumped on the side of the car which luckily had the window open and as the man was small, I reached in to the cab, grabbed his jacket and pulled him out. He seemed shaken but unhurt. By this time the fire brigade had arrived as the station was only a few shops up the road, they sprayed foam all over the car.

It was only that night in bed that I realized what I had done and my thoughts were of horror about how different it could have been.

About one year later I met Maureen who had two children, Alan and Emma, and as it didn't seem that Sue wanted anything to do with me anymore, Maureen and I started seeing each other regularly.

After a while I moved in with her at 31 Ravensroost, Beulah Hill, Upper Norwood. Maureen was a barmaid at the Beulah Spa Tavern at the top of Spa Hill, Upper Norwood. My brother Bill used to be a regular at this pub and I went to have a drink with him. While there I invited Maureen to a barn dance organised by my diving club, we got on very well.

I went to meet Maureen from her work at the Beulah Spa, to find a rather cocky man chatting her up, I didn't mind that until he started to speak very offensively to her. Of course I stepped in and asked him, quite diplomatically, to mind his manners, he responded by saying to me,

"Do you know who I am?"

I then replied, "No, who are you?"

"I'm Roy James!"

"Hello Roy James, I am Martin Bourne and you are being very rude to my friend."

Then all hell broke loose, as he took a swing at me and missed – I always know when to duck – he was accompanied by two very large men who intervened by getting between him and myself and trying to persuade him out the door.

I went back to my pint and continued talking to Maureen when there was a crash behind me and I turned to find he had broken free of his mates and was coming back for more. I picked up a chair and was about to throw it at him, when the two men grabbed him again and tried to leave the pub. The pub manager beckoned to me to jump over the bar and get out the back with Maureen and the other bar staff who had been instructed to do the same, which I did.

I was then told he was one of the Great Train Robbery gang, being one of the getaway drivers and that he was a Formula Two racing driver. He died in 1997 of a heart attack.

About two years after meeting Maureen, we got married on 15 May 1981. I realised after a few weeks that it was probably going to be a fiery life together and a bit strained at times. But what the hell, I would give it my best shot and it was very up and down. Sometimes arguments would start late at night and because I could not sleep on an argument, we would still be awake until the birds were singing in the morning, this couldn't have been good for either of us. Over the course of many years the frequency of these painful and mind-bending altercations decreased. How many brain cells did we lose in these sessions?

Then I found another fill-in job with Abatis, a Pest Control Company, where I had to drive quite long distances to my jobs treating restaurants, butcher shops, and other food companies. When doing a contract at a Little Chef, which is a fast food joint in Rainham, Kent, I had the job of tracing rat runs and then lay baits. I managed to fall through a faulty manhole cover that was hidden in the thick grass, the cover spun around and was wedged firmly across the hole with my legs one each side of it. Lucky for me it was only a shallow manhole, but I still managed to strip the skin off my shin down to the bone. I asked staff at the Little Chef to enter it into the accident book and get the first aider to tend to my shin, out she came and immediately passed out, so I dressed the wound myself. After going to the hospital to check that no blood thinning chemical had entered my bloodstream through my saturated trouser legs, they redressed my wound and said try not to drive for a while. As my job involved a great deal of driving and I found it difficult to drive safely I took a few days off work. Because of that I had a big argument with Abatis, my employer who didn't think I should have had time off and they sacked me, unfair dismissal? Possibly. After their attitude to me I didn't want to work for them anymore, so I went without further dispute.

Now back to a more satisfying job, YMCA Training for Life. They needed a Project Officer, to run a small Carpentry workshop, which was based in a lockup garage at a Youth Club around the corner to the main offices, in Lower Addiscombe Road, Croydon. This was another very exciting and challenging job. Once again I could get to grips with my craft while proving to stretch my people skills even more.

About thirty trainees and I proceeded along with three other members of staff to Hindleap Warren. This was a survival training and character building facility near Forest Row, East Sussex. We had a four night residential course under canvas, by day we would go canoeing, rock climbing, walking – sometimes up to ten miles – also abseiling and orienteering which we also accomplished at night. As in quite a few of my jobs I would say to myself 'and I get paid for this!' We would also go foraging for field mushrooms, edible berries and leaves to add to our evening meal which we had to cook on open fires.

Back to normal days, I was given the freedom to take my group to any public places of interest, museums, libraries, swimming baths etc. So I set a morning per week, if they behaved themselves, for swimming. One of my students only had one arm but I still managed to teach Darren to swim. Two years later I met Darren at South Norwood Swimming Bath by chance, to my surprise he had landed a job as a life guard, I was so proud of him. Again I could feel that dreaded itch from inside my shoes and resigned after just over a year.

After a short hunt for a suitable position, I started with Rentokil, a well-known company in the UK with the Timber Preservation and Rising Damp Department, based at Thornton Heath, Croydon. Here I was employed as a Carpenter Technician which involved cutting out rotten and worm eaten timbers, spraying chemicals and replacing the woodwork and masonry. This involved crawling below floors and in roof spaces, checking and spraying all accessible surfaces of timber. Dry Rot treatment was a big part of our job, most of the time at Rentokil.

I worked alongside Bert Hookins, who actually lived in Perth WA, with his wife and grown up children for five years prior to joining Rentokil. Bert and I had a very big workload, one such job was working at a large school which had suffered a severe dry rot attack. We had to carry many bags of sand which weighed in at well over the cwt or 112lbs, and at least a ton and a half of cement, on top of that hundreds of bricks. Walking up and down six to eight flights of stairs, arriving at the top our legs would almost give out – no wonder I am such a short arse – then running back down stairs like a weight had been lifted – which of course it had – then up onto our shoulders with another burden, back up the stairs again. I would be geeing Bert on as we passed on the stairs, come on Bert I would say on the way down without a load, only another thirty trips and we can start work.

He was a lovely friendly and gentle man, aged about fifty four back then, older than yours truly and had a very high pitched voice as a result of contracting the dreaded diphtheria as a small boy, causing his throat to close up. He had to have a tracheotomy which saved his life but damaged his vocal cords.

It was quite an extraordinary day when Bert and I were given a job in an extremely affluent part the Brompton district of the Royal Borough of Kensington and Chelsea, London, This was an incredibly beautiful building, which had suffered the rigors of an attack by the Dry Rot Fungus, and Bert and I were there to completely eradicate the rot from the house. Luckily we had managed to acquire a police dispensation order which allowed us to park outside the house all and every day due to carrying dangerous chemicals.

On our first day we were greeted by an awfully eccentric lady – for the sake of the story I'll call her Maddy – I would say she was around her early fifties. Maddy took us around her upper ground floor flat through a gorgeous hallway into her large front sitting room with a kitchen area at the rear. The kitchen unit to the right of the sink was falling through to the basement flat below. In the same corner we spotted a standard wooden chair next to this unit and observed that it had rot in its legs with the section of floor beneath it also falling through.

All of Maddy's rooms were thick with household dust excepting where she sat, walked or worked. We could see where she spent most of her evenings on one seat of the big leather couch with piles of books on the remaining two seats and a small low table next to her side with an old fashioned telephone and more stacked books all covered in dust except for the ringer and handset. There were tracks through the dust leading to important areas around the room such as the kitchen, the sink and only part of the draining board were free of the dreaded dust. After Maddy went off to work we started our task in hand, very carefully moving the rotten chair which almost fell apart on lifting it and discovered the floor could not be walked on. We would have surely fallen through.

After talking to the lady in the basement flat and making sure she kept away from this area we soon found the dry rot had travelled all the way down to the basement floor as well. After our first week we found the rot had gone right up into the roof where it had actually started, due to a long term leak. How bizarre it was standing in the basement and gazing up through the holes we had cut through the three floors to see the exposed roof timbers.

At the end of each day's work we spent an hour clearing and bagging up the debris. One evening Maddy came home and exploded at us because we had cleaned her kitchen area, the sink was shining and all worktops and floor spotless! Bert and I were agog after the job we had trying to remove the dust we had made on top of her ten years of greasy dust. Once we arrived at the house when the front door flew open and there was Maddy flapping and fussing around, smartly picked up her briefcase and said, 'I can't stop, I'm in a terrible hurry,' then ran past us down the five steps, tripped and fell forward tucking her head down and completed a forward roll, jumped back up to her feet and ran off like a mad woman leaving Bert and I standing on the front steps with our mouths open in shock and surprise at her extraordinary behaviour.

From Rentokil I was seconded by John who had worked for Rentokil as a surveyor, and now worked for RLH Group where he was a manager. He wanted me to train as a Surveyor with RLH to which I agreed. Soon after I was promoted to Building Manager this I continued until my departure from the company.

One morning Kevin, one of our technicians at RLH, was sent out to drop off some vinyl tiles and adhesive to a house in Coulsdon, Surrey. After about two hours I was wondering where he had got to, then he phoned to say he was in a bit of trouble! Could I come and help? When I arrived at the house, with a sheepish half-smile on his face, he took me to the bathroom where he showed me a swamp of tiles, black adhesive and white spirit all over the floor. I told him he was only supposed to deliver them! His answer to me was that he thought he would show some initiative as he had seen it done many times. Very quickly I had to put this right. This was not an easy job by far. He had used an excessive quantity of adhesive and with tiles sliding around at the touch and overlapping, black glue over the face of the tiles, some of which were white, it took two more hours to finish. The customer was at last happy and had been very good about the whole incident, she even gave Kevin one of her bed sheets, which he ripped up into pieces, to dry things up before my arrival.

A few years later after both Kevin and I had left RLH Group, I saw him in Croydon and he told me that he had started his own building business and called the company 'Happy Builders' with the slogan *If you're happy I'm happy*. I liked Kevin he was a very inoffensive and a happy-go-lucky bloke.

Chapter 20

Our New Home its Ups and Downs

Then the day came after about three years of living in Ravensroost that Maureen and I decided to sell and buy a new home. We sold Ravensroost for the sum of about £39,000. We moved to 1 Queen Mary Road, Upper Norwood. There was a lot of work to do on it but at £27,750 we had plenty of money over. On moving day I had arranged with a different manager for the day off work at RLH Group because my usual manager John was off work with a back problem and I had hired a lorry to move our belongings myself. While offloading our first load I received a phone call from John, to say he didn't know I was having the day off – what a cock up – and that he wanted me to go in to work, I explained,

"I have a van full of stuff to get off and another after that."

He said, "That's not my problem and it is in your own interest to come now."

So I dropped what I was doing to find he had sacked me for not going into work that morning and told me to give him the key to my company car, I asked if I could bring it back when I had done but he snapped back, "No!" How a worm can turn.

I nearly punched the smug smirk off his face – not like me at all – it was a good job he made a very quick exit from my anger and walked out of the office. I took the car anyway because I was 2 miles from home where Maureen and the children were trying to unload the lorry on their own.

Later I was to find out through the proverbial grapevine that John had died.

It was around this time my first grandson Marc was born on May 2, 1986 to my third daughter Maxine.

After a while I took out a family membership with the Independent Order of Foresters, which was an organisation for socializing and holding charity events and pass times as a fraternity. We went on many excursions and joined the rifle shooting club, attached to the organisation, which was very exciting. My daughter Emma and I took away quite a few trophies for shooting .22 calibre rifles. It was quite strange to have two guns and live bullets in my own home – locked away of course – I had been informed that these guns were capable of killing up to one mile away.

Also the two of us went on a sponsored walk for the Foundation of children with Cystic Fibrosis, our walk was 25 miles along the River Thames over the major bridges in London starting at Tower Bridge. We would go from here along the riverside to the next bridge and cross it and so on. Emma and I spent a couple of hours each evening training for two weeks prior to the day. We both found it to be a worthwhile and a good feeling to help these children. The organisers were The Independent Order of Foresters, which we belonged to for a few enjoyable years.

My time at Queen Mary Road allowed me to get to grips
and start many projects at home, some of the most exiting
were growing Bonsai and designing a system of ponds and
waterfalls. These projects grew into a Japanese bridge and
staging for all the Bonsai trees. I also built a new 20 x 12 foot
workshop with a 4 foot deep verandah on the front, with a pan
tiled roof and swinging hammock for relaxing after a hard
day's work. Another construction was an 8 x 9 foot balcony,
9 to 10 feet high outside the first floor rear bedroom, later I
added a staircase down to the garden. It all turned out to be a
little oasis in the heart of town it was so peaceful and relaxing.

After the loss of our young welsh border collie cross called
Oscar, our friends Dave and Jenny found us another of the
same cross breed who we called Badger. He was an extremely
intelligent dog. Badger was to give us at least fourteen
wonderful years of his love and devotion. All our friends and
family got to know him well.

While digging my garden over in the spring of 1987 at Queen
Mary Road, I came across a perfectly round stone about
the size of a pound coin in diameter and ½" thick. When I
showed it to Lesley she insisted it was a button. On cleaning it
I discovered it to be a fossil, so off to Horniman's Museum I
went, to ask them what it was. After about two weeks I had a
phone call to say my fossil and report was ready for collection.
On opening the sealed envelope it stated, 'this item is the
internal cast of the fossil Echinoid (sea urchin) and is at least
160 million years old!'

There are so many undiscovered fossils in the back gardens of
England. I wish I had the chance to dig there again with what I
now know.

It wasn't until I was around 46 that I left the shores of England for another country, a trip to Germany, Asmanhausen to be precise. It was a very emotional feeling when I looked back at the white cliffs of Dover from the deck of the ferry.

Before we set off and were waiting for the coach in Croydon – which would take us to Dover and would stay with us for the entire holiday – I spoke to a young woman sitting on a bench seat, her name was Trudy French and she was extremely charming and friendly. After a few minutes her husband came from parking their car, his name was Peter who was equally as friendly, we chatted away for a short time when a work colleague of Peter and his wife turned up, they were Alan and Pat Sinclair. It transpired that Peter and Alan were both policemen stationed at the Croydon nick. This was to be the beginning of a marvellous relationship which was to last forever.

Maureen and I went on holidays abroad with one or both couples every year, countries like France, Germany, Belgium, Holland, Austria, Spain, Malta, Turkey, Crete, Zakynthos, Corfu, Rhodes, and Cypress, before our marriage broke up. That said Peter and Trudy stayed good friends.

For about nine years so far we email each other as I am now living in Perth, Western Australia.

One day I was walking along Westow Hill, Crystal Palace, and saw a man walking towards me.

As he came to pass me I said, "Roy?"

Looking rather puzzled that I knew his name, he replied,

"Yes."

I repeated, "Roy Carter?"

"Yes"

"Rosendale School around 1950?"

"Well I'll be blowed…who are you?"

"Martin Bourne, we were mates for a while."

After a short pause. "Yes, I remember you now, with your brown and yellow striped jumper pretending to be a bee! And chasing us all over the playground."

"That was me," We chuckled and chatted for a while.

One dreadful weekend when Maureen's Mum and Dad were staying over for a while as their house was being decorated, my son Alan went off swimming in the morning. After about five minutes there was a knock at the front door from a man who had bought Alan home with his chin bleeding profusely. On close examination I could see that there was a one inch split under his chin. He had put his swimming gear bag on the handlebars of his bike and it got caught in the front wheel throwing him over the handlebars. Off to the hospital with him and questions asked with suspicious looks from the hospital staff. This was quite normal in England where children were concerned.

Then on that Sunday I noticed Tess, my mother-in-law running the cold tap over her wrist with copious amounts of blood going down the sink.

"What on earth have you done?" I said with urgency.

"Nothing, I'm alright," she retorted as she turned in order to avoid me looking. I turned off the tap and realized she had punctured the main artery in her wrist with blood actually pumping out, I applied pressure on it and called for Maureen to get a bandage, did my first aid, and took her off to the same hospital we had visited the day before. They gave me the third degree, I think they thought I was beating up my family one by one.

Chapter 21

Finding my Roots

During August 1996 Maureen suggested to me that I search for my natural family, which I did. We went to the family research centre armed with my birth certificate and found the record of my mother's marriage, which arrived in the post about five days later. Next I went to the West Norwood library knowing now that my mother lived in Orpington, Kent around the time of her marriage, I found her phone number. On returning home from the library on August 20, I took a big breath – not knowing what life changing reaction I was about to receive – and made one of the most important calls of my life without a doubt. Hopefully I was about to speak to my mother for the first time in my life.

A lady answered and I asked, "Is that Mrs Osborne?"

She replied, "Yes."

First hurdle over, I said, "Are you alone?"

"Yes."

"You might want to sit down," I continued, "In 1944 on December 3 you had a baby boy."

After a short pause she immediately cut me short and uttered resignedly, "Oh no not that."

That said, I spent one and a half hours talking to her. Some of the questions she asked me were, how tall I was, what colour hair and eyes I had, and was I working. As you can imagine this was an extraordinary moment for me.

She was not happy but I reassured her that all I wanted to do was to let her know where I was and would she let her daughter Janet, my sister, know that I had made contact. She said she would and also that Janet was the only one of her children that knew about me. Her husband had died five years previously, I had two more sisters, Diane and Carol and a brother Clive, who portentously was born on the same date as my birthday twelve years after me, December 3 1956 – this must have been a constant reminder to her not to forget me.

That afternoon I had a phone call that Maureen answered, and she called up to me and said,

"Martin it's your sister Janet."

I said, "I wonder what she wants" as Jane didn't phone much I thought something must be wrong.

Maureen replied, "No it's your sister Janet from the Osborne side!"

I quickly threw a towel around me as I had been in the shower and spoke to the unknown yet familiar person who was in a photo which I had had since I was seven.

She said she wanted to see me and was very emotional, I eagerly asked when, and excitedly she said now! I agreed and a couple of hours later the doorbell rang to announce that Janet and her husband Peter Pankhurst with one of their daughters, Alison had arrived. I felt completely overwhelmed, there were so many tears, with myself included, what an emotional moment it was. The first thing she uttered looking at me and with a look of surprise on her face was 'Oh... Uncle Denis,' he was my natural father.

At one point Janet said,

"You will want to see your father Denis Osborne won't you?"

"Yes" I replied. "I most certainly would."

So she arranged it, and sometime later said she had spoken to my father and told me that he wanted to see me as well. Then the day came when Janet or Jan – as she liked to be called – took me to see him, at the time where he lived, in temporary housing on a local authority caravan site in Wateringbury, Kent.

This was to prove to be another heart-rending and emotional time for all concerned. We were so much alike in looks and temperament, I took one of his hands in mine and looked at it to see if they were alike in anyway. This was the beginning of a very enlightening and soul searching direction in my life, we saw each other many times after that. Sadly he died about

12 years later while he was living in a care home at Poldhu, Cornwall. He was very fortunate to have his step-daughter Barbara and her husband Ray Barber living nearby and making sure he had all he needed. They were wonderful.

After a disastrous end to my last job, I found a job with Budget Timbercare, a timber preservation and damp proofing company, I would start as a surveyor because of my training at RLH. Then I would go on to be Chief Surveyor and responsible for up to six surveyors, finally Manager and second in charge. I was also assigned the task of health and safety officer. I would often go on the tools again for short spells when there were prestige jobs that needed my expertise, one such job was for a small art gallery built in 1902, which was part of Stanley Halls Technical School in South Norwood. This had a very bad attack of the dry rot fungus, which meant a great deal of renovations were needed to the roof and the walls, my boss put me in charge of the whole renovation works. This involved me carving seven timber corbels, twelve ornate plaster corbels, which I cast after making the mould, by applying fifty coats of latex onto the master corbel, also I replicated six elaborate timber beams all for the roof supports.

Martin carving the timber corbels at the Stanley Halls

All corbels and beams reinstated in the Stanley Halls

My boss was extremely good to me and gave me a fairly free rein to run things my way, which I appreciated.

Later I asked Lesley, who was an excellent bookkeeper and looking for a job at the time, if she was interested in working for Budget. As she was, I asked My boss to interview her as he was looking to replace the existing bookkeeper, he consequently employed her. Lesley and I always had an easy and friendly relationship and she worked with us for a year.

Some jobs were not very nice, frankly very unpleasant. What comes to mind was a survey at a house in Tooting, London, where a slightly mental old lady lived as a tenant. I was training a new surveyor and it was to be his first survey, the whole building was filthy. After the survey I had to reassure the tenant about the way we would carry out the work, this would be done in such a way as avoid distressing her too much. So sitting down and facing her I started to explain, she sat on an ordinary kitchen chair, leaning forward with her legs wide apart and almost surrounding a small electric fire. She sat smoking and cooking her private bits! The odour was quite obnoxious as you can imagine.

On my return to the office I was writing up my report when my boss came in and asked, "How did you get on Mart?" as he called me mostly.

My reply was simply, "If you like toasted mouldy old crumpet it was alright."

Then I went on to explain in very graphic detail, more than I dare to explain to my readers. My boss and his partner both cringed and we all ended up in fits of laughter, until I commented, "Just wait till the men start working there and she offers them a cuppa!"

My boss then said, "Martin you must have a whisky after your toxic ordeal."

I then added, "One thing at least, the men can wear their breathing apparatus!"

My boss then poured out a large triple whisky for us. This job had left a nasty taste in my mouth and a whiff in my nostrils, so that was at least neutralized by the whisky.

One of the technicians walked into the office around lunchtime, obviously inebriated, and after making a nuisance of himself I sent him home. He phoned the next morning and gave me a load of abuse and was so clearly stoned that I decided we would be better off without him and I told him to collect his cards when he was more sociable. The next morning he phoned and told me he was coming in to punch my head in! I said, 'Whatever, I'll be here' and put the phone down, half an hour or so later he stormed into my office where three young girls were typing out reports, and two of my surveyors were working. All hell broke loose as he hurled more abuse at me. The girls were getting worried as he continued to goad me into a fight. After swallowing my last mouthful of coffee, I raised myself from my chair, reached for my blazer and calmly said,

"Come with me, we don't need an audience to do this do we?"

I lead the way out of the building, and I might add, around the corner into the next street. Swiftly turning around and facing him I stood firmly on the spot and said,

"Okay, no spectators. Now what do you want to do?"

I noticed he was less under the influence when he replied,

"Is this some kind of a trick?"

I gave him a sincere look and said, "Not at all, we can talk, it's your call. You wanted to punch my head in, you can try I'm equally equipped to do either."

He then came out with something I was not expecting at all and said, "Martin are you ex-military?"

My brain ticked over, "That's the question isn't it?"

He started to talk for about ten minutes or so. While he was chatting on about his problems and me giving him a little friendly advice, I noticed one of my surveyors peeking around the corner. Later I found nearly all my staff had been waiting for a commotion to break out, they were worried, bless them.

I said to the aggressor, "I must get back and you must collect you paperwork and apologise to the ladies."

To which he replied, "Yes I will." After he picked up his cards and apologised to my staff he left, never to be seen again, situation now defused and normal.

While doing some work on Mr Print's shop in Addiscombe Road, Croydon, I noticed a vehicle waiting outside. Sitting in the passenger seat was my pal Dave Godfrey's wife Jenny, I hadn't seen the Godfrey's for many years so I eagerly went up and spoke to her and we exchanged phone numbers. When she looked at my number she said you've only given me my own number back! It tuned out that the last four digits of our numbers were exactly the same 5165, what are the chances of that.

While working with Budget one blustery day in October 1987, during the great hurricane of that year, I went home for lunch. While driving down Wharncliffe Road, Croydon, I saw what looked like a tree swaying and bending in the extraordinarily strong wind about 25 yards ahead. I slowed down then and had to brake suddenly as a massive oak tree came crashing across the road in front of me, I came to a stop only twenty feet, or a couple of cars lengths, from the nearest branches. With my heart pounding in my chest, I got out of the car to check if anybody was around, and after a few minutes of wonder and thoughts of what would have been my destiny, had I been only seconds earlier.

Unfortunately I had no camera. This day was recorded as the worst storm since 1703 and it killed eighteen people, but for a few seconds it may have been nineteen, and this book would have not been written.

Sadly while I was still living in England around 1985, Bert Hookins daughter phoned me to say Bert had had a heart attack and died. I missed him for years after that as he quite often came to our house for dinner.

The boss was always trying to improve his company. One of his ventures was to employ a specialised company – who worked hands on with company owners to permanently secure their business, financial and personal goals – to get involved with us. They were employed to interview and assess every member of staff, including my boss, then submit a survey report.

After this special survey aimed at his staff, including me, one observation of me was and I quote 'Superiors should be wary not to attempt to steal his thunder be it intentional or otherwise' I believe this to be an accurate partial analysis and know it to be true. This survey took six weeks to complete and analysed us in great depth as individuals.

Only about six months after that he came up with a plan, he would start another company using me as one of the directors. I said I would need some time to think on this, I always use the twenty four hour rule.

The next day a meeting was called with all staff, about twenty members. My boss as the chairman asked me if I had thought about his proposition. After seeking advice from a lawyer the day before, I turned down the offer, as he had advised me that I may get into deep water. Well that was another good job gone to the wind, but I wasn't going to be rushed into doing this.

This was a difficult decision to make and during that night I decided to quit. I will not give the reason in this book as it was between my boss and I and will remain private and confidential out of respect for him, as he was a very just and fair man all the time I had known him.

After resigning from Budget, my new job was with CAGU or Community Action Group for the Unemployed. Lesley was working for them, in fact she recommended me to her boss, as I had recommended her to Budget Timber Care earlier. This consisted of retraining people of all ages in a new trade to help find them a job, I held the position of project manager and health and safety officer, which was very satisfying. But the usual problems occurred with drugs and solvent abuse as there was with Community Industry and Training for Life years prior to this.

I heard later after I left, that one of our students who I talked to on many occasions, lost his life. When opening his front door to a gunman brandishing a shotgun he was shot at almost point blank range. His wife and young children were all witness to this terrifying ordeal. Sad but true.

I was made redundant from this job and was told by Lesley afterwards that it was because I had made such a good job of setting up all projects and designing new forms and paperwork that I was no longer needed, mainly because I was on a high salary and had a company car. It doesn't always pay to do your job too well or to be paid a high salary.

While on holiday in Malta with Peter and Trudy one year, we hopped off a bus and with my back to it, heard the sound of its doors closing as it slowly moved off. Suddenly there was crying out and shouting and on turning around I saw a man had his foot caught in the door of the bus with the driver not noticing. I rushed to his aid and held him up off the ground while running myself by this time, I was hoping the driver would see us in his mirror. It was then I noticed Trudy running and shouting to alert the bus driver. By this time Peter was trying to help me with the man. Finally the bus stopped, thanks to Trudy, I couldn't have gone on much longer. The driver opened the doors releasing the foot, and the man was so grateful and he thanked us, then limped away with only a slight scratch on his ankle. Thank goodness that the bus wasn't able to travel very fast due to the traffic. We had lots of adventures with Peter and Trudy.

Trudy is an Aroma Therapist and has a massage treatment room, I had many a good massage from her as she is so professional. I used to marvel at all her certificates lining the wall of the salon.

Chapter 22

Surprises in Store

Around this time, on July 29, 1989 my second grandson, Darren (DJ) was born to my daughter Helen.

My first granddaughter, Holly was born September 26, 1991, to my eldest daughter Sally, although I didn't see her until she was about six months old, as Sally and I have had a very on and off relationship since I left the family home.

My third grandson, Andrew was born February 19, 1994 to my daughter Helen and my fourth grandson, Ben was born June 2, 1996 to my daughter Maxine.

Being out of work once again and after a few weeks of wondering if I was over the hill, I decided the only way was to control my own destiny by starting my own company. Choosing a name suddenly came to me one evening while lying in bed. I said to Maureen 'it's like being on some kind of a crusade', then it struck me 'Crusader' would be a catchy name. After chewing it over for a while I decided it was to be 'Crusader Task Force', and set about planning the whole business. I would start with a feasibility study and check my potential clientele, I created a short questionnaire of just six relevant questions and an information leaflet and took to the streets knocking on doors. Beulah Hill was the first street and in three hours of walking, knocking at doors and talking to people, to my great astonishment I had generated £3,500 worth of work. This was to be started after a short term at a government funded business training programme. Crusader Task Force was born.

I designed brochures and although I had a small amount of advertising, most of my work was on recommendation. My first customer was Mrs Gates and her lovely daughter Gillian or Gill as I called her, who used my services for the duration of my business in England and became very good friends and confidants. Sadly Gill's mum died, a great loss, she was a wonderful lady and we had many tales to tell each other.

It was a great thrill setting up my business, I even wrote a monthly newsletter for all my clients, also gift vouchers every Christmas as a thankyou for their annual custom. This adventure was to last right in to 2002.

I carried out all trades and had a great variety of work which is what I needed. From loft conversions to replacing tap washers, emergency plumbing to roofing, anything to do with buildings or gardens, the smallest and the largest one man could do. I even carried out house removals.

Martin at the wheel ready for a big day and 60 mile (96kms) drive to Littlehampton

When I discovered Friends Reunited, I found my old school mates, one of whom was Roger Cuthbert. It had been forty years since I last saw and spoke to him, he sounded just the same but it would be another five years before I met him again. Corrie and I were visiting the UK when I phoned Roger to see if we could meet again, so all was arranged and we met after forty five years. What a blast it was, apart from being taller with a few wrinkles and a shock of white hair he was still my old buddy Roger, we also met his wife Renie. Sadly the next time we met he was seriously ill but surprisingly cheerful, about a month after that he had died. But we went to see Renie and spent some time with her, hopefully we will be able to see her again one day as she is a lovely person.

Another discovery was my old street buddy Michael Vestey. I was lucky enough to speak to Michael about six months before he died, after he responded to a message I sent via Friends Reunited. I had mentioned his dog Bingo and he phoned me a couple of days later and said with an element of surprise in his voice, "Hello Martin, fancy you remembering my old dog Bingo."

Michael and I talked about the old days which would probably half fill this book. He worked in Fleet Street, London with the Daily Sketch, was a reporter for the Sunday Express and a roving correspondent on the Today programme, he also reported on the Iran-Iraq war in 1980.

Sometimes even though we try to do the right thing, it can back fire on us. Just like the day I was coming home from work along Gipsy Road, I observed an elderly gentleman at the opposite kerb trying to push his wife across this busy road in a wheelchair, so I stopped and jumped out of my van blocking off the traffic and helped the gent to push his wife across to the other side of the road. When we arrived at the opposite kerb and up on to the footpath, the old gent thanked me and I started to go back to my van, but the wheelchair kept falling back to the kerb and he wasn't trying to stop it. I asked him where he wanted to go and with a sorrowful look on his face he very slowly lifted his arm and pointed to the other side of the road where we had just come from!

I smiled and asked him why he hadn't stopped me taking him across the road? He replied that you were being so kind in helping us I hadn't the heart to stop you. Meanwhile all the traffic still held up was waiting for a conclusion to this situation. There was only one thing to do, so I helped him back across the road where we had started, he thanked me and they went on their way. On returning to my van some of the other drivers started clapping and cheering, one man directly behind me was laughing his head off. So embarrassing.

One morning when working for myself, I went to my van and noticed some kind of liquid in the gutter. On further investigation to find its origin, I looked under the van from the road side and observed that something was missing, then it dawned on me! The prop shaft had gone. I tracked the oil drips across and up the road to a point where they stopped, I assumed this was where the thieves had loaded it on to a vehicle. I immediately phoned the police and reported this. After getting a mechanic to fit a new one at the cost of £650, about three and a half day's pay. Two weeks later the police phoned to say they had arrested someone who was trying to sell a prop shaft in a pub, and asked me to identify my prop shaft and give them the serial number! Well of course I couldn't, who even looks underneath your vehicle let alone recognises the part.

They then informed me that the arrest was made on the very day mine went missing and at a pub only 1km from my home but could not let me have it back for reasons I mentioned. Prior to this my van had been broken into three times and my tools stolen, even though I had an alarm fitted which was switched on. When getting the alarm company out to look they said that because my van was quite long, the sensors hadn't detected the rear window being removed. On talking to the police they said they thought someone was trying to put me out of business, probably due to me having at least 35 regular clients in my road alone! You can't win, can you?

In the year 2000 my daughter Emma and husband Les moved to a small village in Cambridgeshire, north of Wisbech called Murrow, we would go and see them now and then but it was a frantic journey through London on an average of three hours long. One day Emma told us that the bungalow next door to her was up for sale. We went to see it and after considering all the pros and cons, including my well established business in London, we decided to move. It meant finding new clientele and while waiting for my work to build up in our new area, I had to travel back and forth to south London where all my past clients stayed loyal to me.

Things were fairly good for a short time while I was doing a lot of work on the bungalow in Murrow. One day I decided to do what I had always dreamed of, that was to have flying lessons. After a trial lesson at Fenland airfield, I booked myself ten lessons, which were fantastic and I carried on until middle of 2001.

When I first took over the controls of the Cessna 152 aircraft it all felt so natural, whether this was due to my extensive use of flight simulators on the computer, I don't know. I think it is easier controlling an aircraft than a simulator as it's certainly more positive. On the ground it feels awkward as you steer with your feet by alternate braking with the left and right brake pedals, once airborne it was smooth and light after trimming for your attitude. Climbing to an altitude of 2000 feet then levelling off, my instructor asked me to shut down the engine's power. After a few seconds, I found the flight controls were getting increasingly sloppy and harder to keep altitude. So I pulled back on the wheel to keep level until the nose dropped. This is called a wing stall due to the lack of air speed. By allowing the aircraft to dive down, the airspeed will pick up, making the controls become positive again. This procedure is known as sacrificing altitude for speed, and of course you can't keep doing this without power, but it was fun and a great way of teaching a novice pilot about the physics of flight.

With the power back on, I practised using the trim wheel, another interesting exercise in flying. This is used for holding the aircraft in a specific attitude i.e. straight and level flight or a steady climb without need of any pressure on the control wheel. I also found landing very natural, granted knowing when and how many degrees of flaps to put on is half the battle. Lining up for the approach and getting the air speed correct is also very important.

Over the landing strip or runway, when almost on the ground, you have to execute the flare. This is achieved by cutting all power and pulling back on the wheel, nice and steady, it's almost like hovering, when the power is cut the aircraft should gently settle like a bird. It was one of the most exhilarating experiences in my life, it felt the same as during my dreams when I would fly. I could write about flying all day. I managed to get my first solo flight in before the time came that I could not afford any more lessons, especially as I needed at least one hundred hours of flying before going for my pilots licence. I was so unhappy about this but work in Murrow was slow moving. I was hoping to start again at some point, but there are more important things in life, I suppose it was a selfish whim anyway.

From one extravagant whim to another, we decided to buy a thoroughbred golden retriever, his name was Brandy. At least he could be enjoyed by Maureen as well and he grew into a beautiful dog and got on very well with dear old Badger.

The dreadful day came where we had the vet come to the house to give Badger the final peace from his undignified illness. While I held him in my arms – he always loved to be cuddled – the vet administered the sleeping draft, Badger gazed at me trustingly, within ten seconds he started to go limp, until after only one minute his ever happy little heart stopped forever. The whole family cried buckets, then up we mustered and went out to the garden. We chose a nice spot and I dug a very deep hole and buried him in my old jumper which he loved and on which he took his last breath. What a dog.

I hadn't been very happy with the way my marriage with Maureen was going, unhappy days were becoming more frequent for quite a time, and I know I tried so hard to make things work. I was always expressing my concerns to Maureen about our lack of communication, she would just reply that she was perfectly content and she may well have been, but I wasn't. We continued to drift apart anyway and I came to the conclusion that I was the only one who could do something about it.

One of my clients was Brenda McDermott and her husband Gordon, who ran a Bed and Breakfast in Crystal Palace, London. They became great friends and after moving to Cambridgeshire I stayed at their B&B sometimes while working in London. I realised that my time on my own in the B&B was so peaceful and without demands. This was all working well for a short time but it only made me realise more how acutely unhappy I was with where my life was going. I felt I was in a deep hole and couldn't get out.

Then one day while at Brenda's I met an Australian lady and in no time at all I had found a soul mate. We talked about everything and anything, laughing all evening long. Her name was Corrie Balcombe from Perth, Western Australia. She only had one more day in the UK and I was due back to Cambridgeshire the next day. I saw her off to the airport and while saying goodbye I tore a ten pound note in half and said, "Take this half, for I hope these two halves will be together again one day." I had no idea how long it would be.

On my return to my home in Murrow, I phoned Corrie in Australia every day for about ten days, until I came to the conclusion that it would be better for both Maureen and I to end the marriage, I felt we had grown away from each other completely.

Although I appreciate that this may have been devastating for Maureen, I felt sure that she would find happiness once more. Self-preservation and survival is a very strong instinct. I also realised that I had to find happiness again, or I would fold up completely, I am well aware that what I was doing was going to be a hard pill to swallow all around but my instincts told me differently.

So I phoned Corrie and said to her,

"If I pay for your return fare back to the UK, would it be a good idea if I came back to Australia with you and see how we get on?"

She still had a month of long service leave from her work. This would give me time to sort out my affairs with Maureen, Corrie agreed and I left home and found a room in Wisbech for two weeks, and with Brenda in Upper Norwood for the remaining two weeks. I did miss Emma and her children when the final break came.

There are two primary choices in life: to accept
conditions as they exist,
or accept the responsibility for changing them.
Denis Waitley

Twenty years from now you will be more disappointed by
the things that you didn't do than the ones you did do.
Anonymous

Chapter 23

A New Life Down Under

After a traumatic time cleaning up the mess I had made, I
finally left England and all I knew, to start a new and very
different way of life in Perth, Western Australia. On our
arrival we were greeted by four of Corrie's mates, all in blonde
wigs with banners waving saying 'Welcome Home Corrie
and Martin' and lots of shouting and cheering – we were like
stars for a moment – Corrie's Mum, Robin was there to pick
us up from the airport. Robin dropped us at the front door of
Corrie's house in Tuart Hill and we settled down jetlagged and
knackered after the long haul.

The next day Robin came and dropped off a small white
sausage of fluff, it was Corrie's little dog Mr Busby, who is
a Bichon Frise/Maltese Terrier cross. Corrie always says he's
like an epileptic toupee, although he is a friendly little dog, I
personally prefer my dogs on the much bigger side.

Now the idea was for me to spend six months with Corrie and
see how I get on over the coming months in Australia. During
the next few weeks I met Corrie's daughter Tarlia and her
partner Anthony. I liked Tarlia from day one, I found her to be
a very happy and friendly young woman and I think we soon

knew what we had to do to get on as a family. Then I was to meet Corrie's brother Richard Ellis and his wife Alison, they too were a very nice couple. I got to know all the people at Corrie's work, where she is a Library Technician at Aranmore Catholic College in Leederville.

The day came when I was invited to join Corrie on a school camp, as she was responsible for driving one of the school buses on this seven hour trip to Kalbarri National Park, This is a very picturesque place with an enormous red gorge, it has Cretaceous and Ordovician formations, also Triassic rock which forms a red bluff. We stayed in a small cabin without a lavatory and unfortunately on the first night I went down with a nasty stomach bug, a very unpleasant experience, but the views there were truly unbelievable.

Corrie and I live in a villa in Tuart Hill – Tuart by the way is a species of a very large tree – and we are a ten minute drive to the nearest white-sanded beach, the beautiful Indian Ocean at Scarborough. The City of Perth is only ten minutes away by car and King's Park is about fifteen minutes from home and overlooks the lovely Swan River. King's Park is mostly natural bush and in the spring and summer produces a mass of wild flowers like, Pink Boronias, Red and Green Kangaroo Paws, Magenta Paperbark trees with masses of creamy white blossom and Orange-flowering Banksias to name a few. On the downside there are extremely poisonous Dugite and Tiger snakes, Redback and Whitetail spiders found around the Metropolitan area.

It was one of the rules of my visa that I had to leave and return to Australia every three months, even for a couple of days, so Corrie and I decided to have a week's holiday in Phuket,

Thailand. This was a great adventure and quite exciting. Back at home Corrie took me out every free moment and showed me all sorts of different places around Perth, I also met her extended family.

It was during this six month period that we planned a trip to Darwin to meet Corrie's father Geoff Bower who picked us up from the airport and also loaned us his car to explore Darwin. Sometimes he would come with us and navigate to places of interest. I loved the climate in Darwin much as I did in Thailand – hot and humid. The crocodile farm was one fascinating place where we fed them, and I held a young one for a while. There were hundreds all around us of all sizes. One place we ventured to near the forest and sat on bench seats, when to my surprise a six foot long reptile came from the undergrowth. It was a Monitor and I tried to get as close as I could to photograph it.

The time came to plan our return to the UK to organize my emigration, so Corrie had to ask her boss for six months off work as she had to come back with me to facilitate a Fiancée Visa. What a long-winded procedure that was and very tiring, taking five whole months to complete and costing a heap of money. We needed proof that we had lived together, so Corrie's brother Richard, his wife Alison, and her Mother all wrote statements saying that we were a couple, the emigration department made it perfectly clear we had to marry within one year of me arriving in Australia. As my divorce from Maureen came through on the 19th December, 2002 there was no problem, we had already arranged our wedding with a celebrant, Jeff Munn, which was yet another condition.

In 2002 on November 11, Tarlia gave birth to Corrie's first grandson, Jaxson, a lovely looking baby and Tarlia was as proud as punch.

Now it was time to return to the cherished country of my birth, England, to sort out my visa, with police clearance, medicals and many visits with the organisation who drew up my emigration plan, also for Corrie to meet my family. One such meeting was with my brother, Bill and his partner Dee, who lived at 106 Rosendale Road, West Dulwich next door to our old childhood home, they both liked Corrie. While there, Bill informed me that his neighbour at 108 – our old house – had asked him about all the buried rubbish in the back garden, knowing he had lived there, as when the builders were excavating the ground they uncovered two motorbikes, lots of old iron bed frames and springs, iron pipes and many other items of household junk. He told Bill there were three skip loads! I believe Bill told him the story of me digging holes in the garden. This rubbish had been underground for forty five years quietly minding its own business, I think they should have called in Time Team!

Most importantly I introduced Corrie to my very precious grownup children, and grandchildren. First to meet her were Helen and Maxine who got on amazingly well with Corrie, to my delight. After a few enjoyable occasions with them it appeared to me that they grew increasingly fond of her, this meant so much to me. Then when Corrie and I went for a drink with my brother Bill, I bumped into Roy Carter again at one of my old haunts 'The Bricklayers Arms' pub in Carnac Street, West Dulwich and we caught up with a few more stories.

Then it was time to return to Australia!

Although Tarlia and Anthony had been together for a number of years, when Jaxson was around six months old they went their separate ways and Tarlia was left holding the baby – if you will excuse my witticism.

Once I had my indefinite resident's visa I could start my business in Australia which I proceeded to do and carried the name from my English business to become 'Crusader Renovations', now I could earn some money again, all that time not earning hit us hard.

That same year Corrie and I got married on October 4, 2003 at Sorrel Park, North Fremantle and Corrie looked beautiful. From here we went to the Red Herring Restaurant on the banks of the Swan River where we had a wonderful meal and company.

Corrie and Martin just married then happily at their reception at the home
of a close friend of Corrie

We would often go off camping at odd weekends or short breaks. One such trip was to a place in the bush called Martin's Tank. On our first night there was nobody there at all where we set up our tent in a small clearing – only about eight metres round – and went for a walk through the bush spotting some of the wildlife that was brave enough to face my camera. Our first night introduced me to a close up sighting, by torchlight, of wild possums when they were frantically trying to recycle our rubbish which was in a plastic bag deliberately hung high in a tree, to keep it out of reach of scavengers! Early next morning I left Corrie sleeping while I gathered some sticks and kindling to start a fire. Corrie commented later about how nice it was waking to the sound of me sawing and chopping wood for the fire with the sun shining through the tent flap. Once the fire was lit I could put the kettle on and make a cuppa to drink while breakfast was cooking. Because the fire was only around three metres from the open tent, Corrie could breathe in the magical ambience of the moment. We stayed here for a couple of nights until a very noisy family pitched quite near us shouting and screaming early in the morning and let their kids bounce a ball all around us without checking them, 'peace had gone from our spot' of all the miles upon miles of bush they had to pick this spot. So we moved on but it was lovely while it lasted.

One Easter we camped at Honeymoon Pool, near Collie where Corrie and I found a perfect camping spot, so we thought. Sometime after pitching our tent Richard, Alison and their boys arrived and we showed them the spot right next to our tent that we had reserved for them. It was time to put the kettle on for everyone while the Ellis contingency endeavoured to pitch there borrowed tent. Now the camping tension began to build as the frustration and flapping started. With their tent finally up, we could relax for a while. After lighting the open fire I swung the barbeque plate over the now raging flames. On with the beautiful beef steaks courtesy of Richard, the smell was gorgeous until the heavens opened, filling the plate with rainwater which started to stew them. Very quickly we all rallied around to salvage our dinner and seek shelter in our tent to sit around the table to finally enjoy our long awaited meal.

Charlie, Andrew and Harry went off to bed and Corrie, Alison, Richard and I could now sit and play cards with our Gin and Tonics while the deluge continued. Bed time for us came all too soon as we were all pretty exhausted so Richard and Alison went back in their tent. But peace was not on the menu for tonight as on entering their tent, they found it was full of water! Yes, their tent was leaking, and on top of that our lovely spot had turned in to a lake. Still belting down, I ventured out to their cries of rain tension with torch in hand and Richard indicating to me – sheltered from the storm of course – where the water was coming in. I ended up being the one getting soaked while banging extra pegs into the ground, as usual in the thick of it. Meanwhile the three boys were trying to sleep on the now floating ground sheet, in places the water was about 8" (20cm) deep. What a night this was!

We expected them to be gone by the morning, leaving all their equipment behind during the night as it was so muddy and soggy after the deluge.

Finally morning was here, all we could think about was packing up our tents and equipment, evacuate the area, and find somewhere nice for breakfast. Richard refused to take the three small foldup chairs as they were wet and very muddy, and he wouldn't put them in his pristine car. So we put them in ours and gave them to our grandkids.

Alison hasn't been camping since and we don't expect she ever will.

Before the deluge, Harry, Alison, Corrie, Andrew and Richard with Charlie and Martin camping at Honeymoon Pool

Ever since I met Richard and his wife Alison, I have always found them to be the most pleasant and fun couple to be with. We have spent so many holidays, evenings, and short breaks together, adventuring and drinking gallons upon gallons of coffee, gin and tonics or wine over a game of mad bridge and picnics. Sometimes just talking, with all the banter we could muster. Please don't let it stop. But hold on – I mustn't forget the fishing on the Frankland River in the boat where I caught my first of many bream, after about fifty years since I had held a rod and even then never caught a fish, not even a scale, well not with a rod anyway. I still maintain that I have caught the biggest fish of us all!

I passed some of my spare time studying Sosai Karate and Aikido for about two years, mainly for fitness and found it improved my all round health, the whole philosophy behind Aikido is particularly intriguing. Unfortunately I had to stop the physical side, due to four of my facet joints in my spine being completely worn out rubbing bone on bone and causing great pain. This was due to my very heavy and active working life.

I only found out what was causing it when I spent nearly two weeks walking with a stoop because of this aggravation. I was working on a job at that time laying paving slabs and had to finish it, enduring the agony, or wait two months before getting paid as the customer was off to Italy and wanted to see the job finished before settling up with me.

It's only been the last six or so years that I now admit to, and can put a definite name to, a problem I have suffered from way back into my mid-twenties. This terrible affliction is known as panic attacks and night terrors, where I feel like I am going to die, with my heart pounding, leading to the shakes and cold sweats, also a sense of impending doom, this sometimes happens in the day as well and is very debilitating. Most of the time I have felt as strong as an ox and could fight an army, but while experiencing these attacks I feel I am reduced to a weak, helpless wreck. Over the last four years I have developed some mental tools to combat this which come into play, once I recognise the symptoms, these help to fight it off and they do most of the time.

I hope that anyone reading my book will get some benefit from my experiences.

Chapter 24

New Interests and Travel

In 2010, I stated to build a scale model of a World War II
Lancaster Bomber out of plywood and aluminium which
will have a one metre wing span when completed. There are
over one and a quarter million parts and nearly two million
processes, a long job but who's hurrying. With the tiniest parts
involved and the detail needed in the painting of the dials and
small parts, I am so thankful that I have spent most of my life
working with my hands and so grateful that my dexterity and
eyesight is as good as ever.

It is wonderful being retired. I am relishing it. Quite a number
of years ago I decided to learn to sing properly, I love Italian
Arias, and after a few months of practising at home by
learning many songs phonetically and listening to a given
song hundreds of times. For one Christmas Corrie gave me a
present of a singing lesson which I enjoyed but the voice coach
was too expensive at $60 an hour. She did however confirmed
that I was predominantly a tenor and could sing down to low
baritone and high bass.

Later I found another voice coach who was an elderly
gentleman named Laurie Russell who was more affordable

at less than half the cost, which allowed me to have at least one lesson a week. One day Laurie said to me, knowing I was a builder, would I like to do a few jobs on his house for him instead of me paying him, this worked very well. By 2012 he was too ill to teach but I still visit him once a week to get him some shopping and do a few odd jobs for him. After a few weeks of singing with Laurie he wanted me to audition for a production of 'The Pirates of Penzance'. So I went along for my audition – which was a nerve racking experience – and took my place in front of three judges. I sang 'Torna a Soriento' and two weeks later I received a phone call from the Gilbert and Sullivan Opera Company inviting me to join them for three months of rehearsals which I attended and I thoroughly enjoyed the whole experience. I then went on to perform my part at the Playhouse Theatre in Perth City, there were seven performances over four days.

Half an hour before going on, we had to mingle with the audience in the booking office and the foyer without interacting and acknowledging them, as if we were spirits of famous people from the past. This was a little nerve racking but exciting at the same time. My part was to play Sir William Gilbert as a singing spectator, hypothetically watching the opera and singing with the gallery chorus. In the meantime I was still occupied with my Italian songs which I still practice several times a week, around forty to forty five arias to date.

On another occasion I was asked by the Perth Oratorio Choir, as they were short of tenors, if I would rehearse and perform with them the well-known Handel's Messiah at St Andrews Church in Perth on Christmas Eve, once again I agreed.

Then it was time to leave the heat for what turned out to be eight and a half months in my beloved England.

Months before leaving Australia for the UK my very good friends Dave and Jenny Godfrey insisted that we stay with them for a while and of course we agreed, they have a wonderful home in South Godstone, Surrey, with a small lake and a boat in their back garden, what a dream. About a month before leaving Perth, Dave sent me a photo of what he called our new home, he had gone to all the trouble of converting his loft area into a bedroom for us, it was so exciting. After Corrie and I arrived in the UK, Dave kindly picked us up from the airport as we had planned to purchase a cheap car for the duration of our holiday and we hoped to stay for one year. We left South Godstone after about three weeks and stayed with Brenda McDermott in her new home/B&B, at Babbacombe Road, Bromley in Kent. While using this as our base we spent two weeks at her holiday home in Shanklin on the Isle of Wight, staying in the ground floor of the cottage while I rebuilt the balcony for her. This was in great need of repair and led out from the second floor flat which she let out on a permanent basis. The money she paid me gave us the necessary funds to make our holiday more comfortable, and free accommodation to boot.

While there, we were having lunch at the Hideaway Cafe on the cliff top when I said to Corrie, after hearing a man talking to Mick the cafe owner,

"That man is from South London." With that I decided to speak to the man and said,

"You're from South London aren't you?"

"*Yus* mate, West Norwood," he replied.

Taking note of his age I said, "My Mum and Dad lived over the old oil shop in Norwood Road, they were burnt out during the war."

He immediately replied, "What's your name mate, Bourne!"

"Yes! What's yours?"

"Beecheno."

Astounded I said, "Beecheno, the only person I knew with that name was Ronny."

"That's me!" he said with an exited look on his face as he studied my face more seriously.

This caused a whole session of reminiscing. He remembered seeing Uncle Ken's RAF aircraft transporter standing outside our house and talking to him on occasions. After chatting to Ronny for a while, we took names and addresses. Ronny and his Dad Arthur were both postmen and well acquainted with our family. I knew his Dad as Uncle Arthur, when they lived in Eastmean Road, around the corner from us. Before we left the Island we went to see Ronny again at his home where he made us a cuppa and chatted for a couple of hours, we have since emailed each other a few times.

Apart from my grown up children and their families, when staying in England we would visit my half-sister Jan, half-brother Clive and their families a few times and we would catch up with all the gossip. We also looked forward to spending a few days to a week, a couple of times, with my cousin Rick Doyle from the Osborne side of my family. Rick always said we were welcome at any time, and is one of the most friendly and obliging people I know, we were also very fond of his Mum, Aunt Bubs or Dorothy, who was a very kind person with a terrific sense of humour, we both miss her. Rick is also an extremely talented carpenter and used to make unusual longcase clocks. We have been to many places of interest with him to name but a few Bodium and Dover Castles, Eltham Palace and lots of National Trust or English Heritage establishments. Rick is a very interesting and empathetic personality, a thoroughly good chap all round and we always looked forward to sharing laughs and staying with him on our visits.

While we were staying at Brenda's in 2009 we met a family from Germany staying there, Jonny and Isabel Capuana and their daughter Tanya. I was talking to Tanya one day and mentioned Corrie's ancestors who came from a small village in Germany in the mid 1800s. I informed her that it was a place – not expecting her to know it – called Steinheim an der Murr. Tanya said – with a deal of surprise on her face – that she knew it well and sometimes did work there – as she is a journalist and her base is in the closest main town of Marbach. Later when talking to Corrie, Tanya said she would like to write a story for her newspaper about Corrie's quest to find information about her ancestors. We booked a holiday in Steinheim when Tanya was back in Germany and she took us to meet the local genealogist and historian Hans Deitl. He showed us all around the village, including where Corrie's ancestors had lived, a large museum and the church where her family were christened and married. It was the most fascinating and quite mind blowing journey through time.

At this time we travelled north to Wisbech, Cambridgeshire to visit Mick and Bridget Hughes who live near Gedney, Lincolnshire. We caught up with any news and had a wonderful dinner in the evening at their home. Mick had a computer shop on the market square in Wisbech. We stayed at a B&B in Union Place, owned by Janet Stott who became a good friend to Corrie and I in the years that followed. We also stayed at Sue Harman's B&B for a couple of nights near Mick's house. While here we went to a little village called Tittleshall in Norfolk to pay a surprise visit to my old friends Tony and Christine Smith, who I hadn't seen for thirty years.

We arrived at Tittleshall where they had lived with their three children when last I saw them. I knocked at the door and after a few seconds there he was, standing in the doorway with a second's puzzlement on his face, called out my name and wrapped his arms around me then quickly invited me into his home, at the same time trying to call out to his wife, Chris. It's Martin! What a welcome! After introducing Corrie, we had a lovely catch-up and talked our heads off all afternoon. Another delightful experience. They then asked us to come and stay for a few nights but regrettably we had run out of time and had to make tracks back to dear old London where my children and grandchildren were waiting to see us one more time before our return Down Under.

On our next trip to Europe, my sister Jane and her partner John kindly treated Corrie and I to their holiday home in Tuscany, Italy for a week. This was to prove an interesting change of scenery and company. Jane and John took us to a couple of neighbouring towns, it was a pleasure to catch up with Jane after quite a few years. We travelled to Anghiari, a walled town set high on a cliff-like mountain, nothing appeared to have changed since the eleventh century. We got to see the source of the Tiber River and loved the difference of strolling through a local market compared to an English speaking one. While driving there we spotted our first sighting of a porcupine on the hillside, it was surprisingly large, as big as a shopping trolley! We were so lucky to be able to get a taste of such a breathtaking country.

While in the UK, we caught up with an old friend of mine that I had found on Friends Reunited. I hadn't seen or spoken to Mick Rice since I was 17, and it was so fabulous to see him again. What was fascinating was the way we both recognised each other immediately, as he was outside his house talking to a neighbour when we arrived. Before meeting him, Corrie asked me who Mick looked like, I said, Liam Neeson the actor came to mind and sure enough when meeting him Corrie agreed and told Mick what I had said. Corrie thinks that he even speaks like him but with a different accent.

On our return to Australia we learnt that Tarlia had met up with Mike Byrne, who she hadn't seen since they were at school together, they had started going out and were a serious item by then. They soon realized it was the right time to add to their family and Jaxson was looking forward to having a long awaited brother. Tarlia gave birth to Kyden on April 5 2011. She didn't have an easy time but everyone was over the moon with his arrival.

Now time to get back to my swimming at the Terry Tyzack Aquatic Centre, as usual I got talking to someone! Steve Doughty who works as a carer for a group of mentally challenged people. He became a very good friend and I meet him at least once a week at the pool. Steve sometimes has five clients with him in the pool and I join in with keeping them occupied. I admire Steve's unselfish manner with his clients and they all seem to like him. It takes a very special kind of person to cope with this sort of work and he is well suited to it. We always have many stories to talk about, also everyday problems are discussed and I think we both get some benefit from these little chats.

Then in February 2012 Robin Ellis, my mother in-law, saw a newspaper item asking for gentlemen to join an A Cappella chorus called 'Men in Harmony', so off I went to see what they were like and joined in. After a few weeks I had an audition and was accepted as a lead singer. I have now been on many gigs including Christmas Carols on the streets of the City of Perth. Sadly I had to give it up after only fifteen months or so, I miss the other guys especially Ross Rhodes and Ron Shaw but I do see them occasionally when we go and have a coffee together which is always enjoyable.

In the eleven years I have been in Australia, my dental health has suffered greatly. After holding on to a pair of crowned back teeth for at least fifteen years, they finally worked loose and eventually came out when I had only been in Australia for two years and couldn't afford dental care, $3500 to be exact! After sending an email to my very good friend Trudy French who lives in the UK and used to be a dental nurse, what I could use to fix them back, she sent me the formula of Potassium Sulphate and Clove Oil mixed together to make a putty-like cement. So off I go again playing the dentist, only on myself of course, cleaning out the cavity and mixing up the compound, pushing the crown firmly in place and biting down for a minute then cleaning off the surplus cement – job done. This time the crown stayed firmly in place for over a year.

On our last trip to England in 2012, Peter and Trudy French invited Corrie and I to stay for a couple of nights with them in their home in Exmouth, Devon. We had two wonderful nights and three days with them, this was the first time they had met Corrie and they both liked her, well who wouldn't like Corrie. It was only a few days after this we stayed with Tony and Chris Smith, as they had invited us to do on the previous visit to the UK.

We spent two wonderful nights and three days in their company. They drove us to various places of interest, I don't think we stopped talking as there was so much to catch up on. Chris took us to Gressenhall Farm and Workhouse where she had worked at some point in her thirty odd years of living in Norfolk. While Chris and Corrie were getting to know each other, Tony and I were reminiscing and having a bit of technical chatter here and there. Chris made us some interesting and very tasty breakfasts and evening meals, it was so thrilling to spend so much quality time with my old friends from yonks ago.

In early November 2013 we were quite surprised when Corrie's brother Richard put a proposal to us, as he had to up and move his whole family to Melbourne due to his job commitments. He put it to us to consider if we would be prepared to move close to his and Corrie's Mum in Nedlands to be available for her if she needed us.

We agreed and after all the packing and dramas concerned with moving house including looking for a suitable rental house in the right price range, was a task on its own. Finally, we found a triplex in Dalkeith Road, Nedlands, and moved in on December 27, 2013. After settling in and my dear Corrie back at work, poor girl, I could plan my time whilst on my own. Back to writing this book was a priority of course and I soon found myself regularly spending many hours at the best of the best cafés in Nedlands – Martineau's Patisserie – the owners are Christian and Christine Martineau, both very friendly people and their superb staff Nielie, Di the Princess, Tina, Lorraine, Becky and Maddy all work so well together, I have never seen such affable teamwork in a café. All manner of pastries, cakes and meringues galore, some unique to the owners. It is such a great environment to concentrate on my endeavour – my writing of course.

May 28, 2014 at 8:30am I finally had two teeth extracted that had been a worry for the last twelve years. As it had been nearly 50 years since my last extraction, I had forgotten what a horrible feeling it was having my jaw yanked at with the crunching sound and the aftermath of pain and strange feelings as the anaesthetic wore off.

Later that day I had a serious car accident and had a severe seatbelt injury to my chest including broken ribs this made coughing, sneezing and hiccups during the next eight weeks exceptionally painful. The car was a write-off, so away we went hunting for another car about a week later, during this quest, with her eyes pinned on a potential car, Corrie fell in a pothole in the road next to a car yard and broke her foot. After a few days she went to hospital for x-rays and they fitted her with a moonboot, so she couldn't drive for about eight weeks. What a dreadful time that was too. All in all it took us quite a few months out of our year to recover.

Chapter 25

About My Children

You don't have to see or be with your children
For you to love them!
When the thought of them comes into your mind
with a warm glow that fills your whole spirit.

MB

Monday's child is fair of face

My first daughter Sally. Sally was born at the General
Lying-In Hospital, Westminster Bridge Road in London. I
wanted to be at the birth but was sent away after being told to
go for a drink as she wasn't due yet. Only 20 minutes later I
returned and Sally had already been born! I was so annoyed
with the staff for packing me off. Sally is a very creative and
friendly person with a strong will. Once when she was quite
young, she leant across the kitchen table and trapped her arm
in between the spout and the body of an aluminium teapot of
freshly made tea. This left a nasty burn on her little arm and
we rushed her to Dr Skinner straight away but it still left a
scar for quite a while. On another occasion she managed to get
a small bead stuck in her ear, off to the hospital to remove it
we went. When she was between eight and eleven she would

love to do acrobatics with me and soon learnt to balance on my shoulders without holding onto me. Sally has provided me with a lovely granddaughter Holly and now Holly has given me my first great grandson, Riley, who I have yet to meet. Sally and I have had our differences which didn't help at all when Sue and I split up but she is still my child and I love her dearly.

Friday's child is loving and giving

My second daughter Helen. Helen was born at our home in Clive Road, West Dulwich while I was at work and I didn't get to see her birth either. Helen is a sweet-natured, sensitive person, devoted to her children. She has a great sense of responsibility and always has a beaming smile whenever I see her. When Helen was very young, she was with Sue while Sue was working at someone else's house. Helen somehow managed to get a peanut stuck right up inside her nose and the only thing I could think of at the time was to put some pepper on her top lip and block off the opposite nostril. We waited for her to sneeze, seconds later she did and outshot the offending nut. Helen has given me two wonderful grandsons Darren (DJ) and Andrew (Andy). I love them both and enjoy their company very much and we always have a laugh on our all too infrequent visits.

Tuesday's child is full of grace

Number three daughter Maxine. Maxine was also born at Clive Road and I was most certainly there this time. Maxine is an extremely loving and affectionate person with a great sense of humour. As a little girl she would come running down Clive Road – where we lived at the time – to meet me from work, legs and arms going everywhere. I love all my children in different ways, one thing I will never forget with Maxine is bringing her into the world with my own hands. Maxine has achieved so much with her further studies and she has given me the pleasure of two terrific grandsons Marc and Benjamin (Ben), who we see and spend some time with when we visit the UK about every two years, I can't but love them all.

Monday's child is fair of face

As for my fourth child and first boy, I left the family home when he was only 5 and I never really achieved a proper bond with Martin Lee or Lee as I called him – to save confusion within the family – he is my youngest child, and I'm sad to say that he now sees me as a total stranger. Even though I have seen him from time to time at most ages and there didn't appear to be anything wrong. He is entitled to his own feelings, but he is still my son and I will always love him as such.

One thing I do know I didn't know my natural father at all, and was adamant that I never would.

Can one person categorically say they don't like another and truly believe it if they don't even know anything about them? But believe me age changes your perspective on life, it certainly did with me and after meeting him as a perfect stranger when I was 54, I got to know him as a person and I could see something of him in me which I found enlightening. I liked his company. I found my natural father Denis to be a sensitive, gentle man with a similar sense of humour as me. This has in no way, shape or form changed my feelings towards my Mum and Dad, who gave me a home at such a young age, as they will always remain enormously special human beings.

Chapter 26

Reflections Past and Present

I always looked for and managed to find something extra to do in my life at all ages. Among my never ending hobbies are model making, mainly aeroplanes, including three flyable models. I had lots of fun flying them over Mitcham Common until one crashed into the top of a very large tree. I have spent hundreds of hours wood carving, many of these were animals and some abstracts. Another interest was photography, I learned how to develop negatives and prints and found it magical the way a blank sheet of paper gradually transformed into a perfect picture. There were no digital photos or cameras then, it was all painstaking work with chemicals and specially coated paper. Electronics was another fascination, from basic components I made instruments like dampness indicators, amplifiers, sirens, wirelesses and more. I loved my swimming, and my long stint at sub aqua diving but flying light aircraft was the supreme pleasure, and I could go on.

Over the years I have realised that I was educating myself with the things I liked doing, I must have read hundreds of instruction and operating manuals. Reading some of these manuals was exceedingly hard going with my word identification disability but I had to persevere if I wanted to achieve my sometimes almost unattainable aspirations. This all helped me with my reading ability, especially in the workplace. I still struggle to this day as words jump around in my head and on some days – not too often now – it is almost impossible to make any sense of my reading, so writing is a colossal task but tremendously rewarding and I might add enjoyable. Due to these difficulties I found that I had an empathy with others, and had a natural ability to pass on my skills to people who had similar problems.

If anybody thinks that because you are getting old and maybe retired, that this means the end of inspiration and ambition, this couldn't be further from the truth. If you summon up an interest and work with it, and don't worry, if nothing comes of it, try something else. Most of my important ideas and adventures, have come to me in the last thirty odd years. My feelings are that you must not stop trying new things in your life. Being retired gives me more time to explore other ventures, but of course along with retirement goes less money in the bank.

I have always been a self-motivator and soon learned from an early age to lead rather than follow, if I could. Although there have been times where I have recognised that someone was a stronger leader than me, in these cases rather than just following, I have developed more of a team building attitude. I do believe that this attitude helps to generate more interests in your life when at work or play, and even when you retire. I have always enjoyed talking and listening to all sorts of people, and felt that it was the most sincere way to communicate with feelings and passion. All the years of being afraid of the pen and proverbial blank sheet of paper, has held back a great deal of words, until now finally I find myself bursting with the desire to write, and the more I write and think the more it makes way for the backlog of thoughts and memories still locked away in the old grey matter.

Quite a while after starting my manuscript, I was having a coffee in a café book shop, called the Bodhi Tree, on the corner of Oxford Street and Scarborough Beach Road, Mount Hawthorn, when I spoke to a lady who was selling books. As usual I got chatting and lo and behold she happened to be a published author! Her name is Elizabeth Bezant and she has been so helpful by giving me the odd tip here and there, I have also read a couple of her very edifying books on authorship assistance. It was so nice to meet a professional person who was warm and sincere, Elizabeth may your future shine on you.

My Dreams and Nightmares

In my early teens I had the most terrifying dreams and nightmares. One such nightmare would recur many times. I was being chased, and as fast as I ran the pursuer was always there, I would shut doors behind me but the doors were too small for the openings and would flap back and forth through the openings like swing doors, nothing I did seemed to work although he never caught me, but it was a close thing and left my heart pounding. My assailant was 'Gill-man' from the film, 'The Creature from the Black Lagoon' – look him up on the web. He was so scary that I would stay awake in case he returned to my vivid dreams, then I had an idea that before I went to bed I would approach all the doors in the house, and shut them one by one and held the handle for a minute until I decided to open them on my own terms. I only had that dream once more and sure enough the doors stayed shut and that was the end of that nightmare and the dreaded monster 'Gill-man'.

In some dreams I found myself in charge of a troop of soldiers, with guns and grenades going off as they do, sometimes with weird twists to them. Very often friends or family members came into it, my mission was to rescue them and I always seemed to manage somehow. I was forever saving people, my theory for this is that for years I wanted to join such organisations like the Fire Brigade or Ambulance Service but they were too fussy about height or academic training. I know I could have done both well. I still have many extremely twisted dreams, I could almost write another book about my dreams, as I nearly always talk about them when I wake. I have spoken to many people about the subject, and I would say that most have said they either don't dream or can't recall their dreams.

Sometimes when I have time to daydream, I think of the people who are no longer with us, i.e. Mum, Dad and Lesley, even Uncle Alec. Such thoughts as how Dad would have felt about personal computers, and the progress made with mobile phone technology and the internet, I'm sure he would have surfed the web. The older I get the more I wish I could talk to them in person and show them even more appreciation for their care and interest in my wellbeing. I have so many questions to ask about their lives although I was always asking while they were alive, except now I have different and more poignant subjects to discuss and thoughts to share. I miss sharing my philosophies with my family even though sometimes we would get bogged down with family politics. I must just add that for many years even after I married and had my own family, I did feel under an enormous amount of pressure to prove myself, in the main, to my older sisters. That pressure is all but gone thank goodness.

I have enjoyed my life so far and hope to have many more exciting years to come, the decisions I have made haven't always been easy by any means, I'm sure I have hurt people in my very nearly 70 years on this Earth, certainly unintentionally. If I have I'm not proud of that at all. I must admit that apart from growing up dramas and traumas, my life has been a playground of learning which is still ongoing. I love all nature, people included, but I find modern society with all its red tape and outdated rules can be a vexation to my spirit.

Rules are for the guidance of wise men
and the strict obedience of fools:

This quote I believe is attributed to Harry Day, an English
First World War fighter ace.

Of course I'm aware that we need some modern things today,
certainly when we become very old or if we weaken. I would
like a wilder form of living with a more ancient form of stress,
if the truth be known, as I know I have a natural survival
instinct which seems to kick in when needed. I have come to
learn that a great deal of the ills we suffer are due to not being
able to react to our natural feelings in modern society.

On the other hand modern technology is moving so fast and
it is one of my great fascinations to see just how far it will
evolve the human mind and condition. I have dived the deep
oceans and flown the skies and travelled to many countries,
now I would like to stand on the moon and observe the
place of my birth from afar. I hope to see my great-great-
grandchildren gazing in amazement at the world we live in
with all its surprises and things to learn, hopefully getting a
distance from modern technology now and again and seeing
the earth for what it really is. Oh to have better vision. I seem
to have less time now I am retired than when I was engaged
in my full time work, although I can now take my time in
whatever I want to do and more or less choose when I do
things. Of course this is only possible because of my lovely
hard working wife, Corrie. I'm living a fairly selfish life at
present which is not easy to admit.

My Australian family is growing now as on August 15 2014, Tarlia gave birth to her third baby, Tarlia and Mike have named him Tyson, now she's got her hands really full.

I haven't seen my family and friends in England since June 2012 and I am missing them like hell, now it is time to return to my beloved England. The plan is return for one month, as that is all the time Corrie has off work for Christmas 2014. After three years of retirement I have to go back to part time working for myself. I think it must have been written, as on February 18 at my new café haunt Martineaus, a lady approached me and said, "Hello Martin."

It was Jill Simon, a client of mine from at least four years ago, she asked if I was still working. I said, "No but for you I will, what do you need?" She told me she needed some serious tree surgery carried out on a number of trees and other odds and sods. It was a good job that I was walking or cycling every day to get my fitness back.

I often have a chuckle to myself when thinking that all my life I have had an idea in my head that one day I would do something extraordinary or become famous, for some such reason or another, although I have had my moments. Where this comes from I haven't a clue but even now it is still there. Years ago I would not have told anybody about this, let alone write it in a book for all and sundry to read. I have always been a person to speak my mind, as many of my bosses have found to their displeasure! Making waves has been my forte and I still make them and probably will till I draw my last breath. For I believe that most of the time there is a positive reaction to shaking things up as it inhibits stagnation and encourages more vigour and passion as a rule, in my opinion.

Epilogue

If you have read this far there must have been some interesting chapters in my book unless you have jumped a chapter or two. I can't believe a life story can in every part be a feel good read as there is always uninteresting or even downright boring scenarios in everyone's life. I have tried not to be too boring. I would like to believe that in 20 years from now I can write a follow up to this although it would be a shorter book, only if this is moderately successful, we will see. The people in my life have on the whole been kind, but occasionally there have been some real stinkers. Most of my adventures have been beneficial, even the dangerous escapades, as I'm sure if you have half a brain you will learn something or another no matter how small.

I could have gone on for an eternity editing adding and subtracting sections of my book but my fear is that many aspects of my character will be lost the more I delay publication so I must bite the bullet as they say.

If you try to polish anything for long enough eventually
you will have nothing left of the original.
Knowing when to finish before all character
has been expunged is the secret,
As perfection is not to be had in this life

MB

Houses where I lived

Addresses	Years
108 Rosendale Road, West Dulwich	1944-1954
3 Morton Hse Bentons Ln W Norwood	1954-1956
108 Rosendale Road, West Dulwich	1956-1963
Tritton Road, West Dulwich	1963-1965
167 Gipsy Road, West Norwood	1965-1966
Clive Road, West Dulwich	1966-1980
49 Lancaster Avenue, West Norwood	1980-1982
31 Ravensroost, Upper Norwood	1982-1986
1 Queen Mary Road, Upper Norwood	1986-2000
Orchards, Back Road, Murrow, Cambs	2000-2002
Lawley St, Tuart Hill, WAustralia	2002-2013
Dalkeith Road, Nedlands WAustralia	2013-2015

Some of my Employers from 1960-2010

C F Palmers, Brixton	Apprentice	1960 1½yrs
Advance Laundry, Norwood	Van Boy	1961 4 wks
H Day & Sons, West Norwood	Removals Porter	1961 1 yr
Humpfreys, Crystal Palace	Building Labourer	1962 4 wks
Tersons, Bermondsey	Labourer	1962 5 wks
Kineer Moody, Oxford Circus	Miner	1962 3 wks
Wyatt's, Crystal Palace	Building Labourer	1962 4 wks
Baths Buildings, Herne Hill	Carpenter	1962 6 mth
General Builders, Clapham	Carpenter Handyman	1963 3 mth
Halse & Sons, West Norwood	Building Labourer	1963 5 wks
T Brown & Sons, Herne Hill	Carpenter/Joiner	1963 1 yr
Southwark Counc., West Dulwich	Carpenter/Joiner	1964-1965
H Dale & Son, West Dulwich	Boot Repairer	1965-1966
Lambeth Council, Upper Norwood	Carpenter/Joiner	1966 6 mth
R E Moate & Co, Beckenham	Carpenter/Joiner	1966-1968
Self Employed Builder, W Dulwich	All Trades	1968-1972
Envoy, Leytonstone	Driver/salesman	1972-1973
P J Heard, West Dulwich	Carpenter/All trades	1973-1974
Masons Timber, Herne Hill	Driver/Yard Sales	1974 6 mth
P J Heard, West Dulwich	Carpenter/All trades	1974 4 mth
Reliance Security, Tulse Hill	Patrolman to Inspector	1975-1976
ILEA, Loughborough	School Bus Driver	1976
Grove Coaches, West Norwood	Coach Driver	1977
Community Ind., Battersea	Scheme Consult.	1977-1979
Abatis, All Over	Pest Control Technician	1979 3 mth
YMCA Trainer, Croydon	Carpentry Instructor	1980-1981
Rentokil, Thornton Heath	Carpenter/Plasterer	1981-1983
R L H Group, Crystal Palace	Surveyor/Manager	1983-1985
Budget Timber, Thornton Heath	Surveyor/Manager	1985-1988
CAGU, Croydon	Project Officer	1988-1989
Crusader Task Force, U Norwood	Own building business	1989-2002
Crusader Renovations, Tuart Hill, WA	Own building Business	2003-2010
Retired, Tuart Hill, W Australia	Rest	2010-now

Photo Credits

Bedford Ox Tractor Unit and Queen Mary Trailer page 22
© Copyright Richard Hoare and licensed for reuse under this
Creative Commons Licence

Crystal Palace Transmitter Page 54
by Mark Ahsmann. This file is licensed under the Creative
Commons Attribution-Share Alike 3.0 Unported license.

Front Cover background photo south coast Western Australia
by Martin Bourne

Back Cover Photo Tower Bridge over River Thames
by Martin Bourne

Front Cover Portrait
by Corrie Bourne

Sketches of Martin on page 49
by Janet Fullman nee Bourne